920.02
Se82i **Seventeen.**

In my opinion; the Seventeen book of very important persons. New York, Macmillan [1966]

211 p. ports. 21 cm.

1. Autobiographies.   I. Title.

CT101.S393   920.02   66–29556
                                                      495

In My Opinion:
The **seventeen** *Book of Very Important Persons*

In My Opinion

The seventeen Book

of Very Important Persons

THE MACMILLAN COMPANY, NEW YORK

COLLIER-MACMILLAN LTD., LONDON

Library of Congress Catalog Card Number: 66-29556

First Printing

The Macmillan Company, New York
Collier-Macmillan Canada Ltd., Toronto, Ontario
Printed in the United States of America

Dear Teen-ager:

An astonishing variety of celebrated people wrote the chapters of this book. The authors are folk singers, statesmen, scientists, actors, novelists, businessmen, musicians, doctors, painters, educators and playwrights. What they have in common is that each of them cares deeply about you. You will find no posturing or pretense or pontification in these pages, for these adults have scaled the wall that separates the generations and have written with searching honesty, warmth and good will. They chose their own subjects, writing about what concerns them most or what they think concerns teen-agers most. This brought a number of revealing surprises, but I will not spoil your enjoyment by giving any of them away here. I want you to discover for yourself the real persons behind these famous names and faces.

Opening this book is rather like walking into a large party with every guest a celebrity, and all of them eager to talk just to you. *SEVENTEEN* is proud to serve as host—and I'm sure you'll have a lively, inspiring and happy time.

Most sincerely,

Enid A. Haupt

In My Opinion:
The **seventeen** *Book of Very Important Persons*

VANCE PACKARD

The Girls That I Cherish

Vance Packard set the whole country talking with two best-selling sociological books, The Hidden Persuaders, *which deplored the use of motivational research in advertising as an invasion of privacy, and* The Status Seekers. *His most recent book is* The Naked Society. *He was born in Pennsylvania and worked his way through college and graduate school. He is married and has three children, and is also the co-author of* How To Pick a Mate: The Guide to a Happy Marriage.

Today the challenge of being an effective person—girl or man—is in some ways becoming more and more difficult. All of us, and especially younger people, are subjected to enormous pressures both from our environment and from professional persuaders to pattern our lives in ways supposedly appropriate for the group or social class to which we become attached. We are under pressure to strive constantly to make what is believed to be a good impression, to be or seem clever, to acquire the status symbols our peers and elders esteem.

This problem is much on my mind now, perhaps, because I am the father of a daughter and two sons. The pressures on girls are in many ways, I believe, more severe than on boys because in our society girls are encouraged to be more preoccupied with the impression they make. But I have long pondered the matter of the traits that are important in young people. (Few people remember it but fifteen years ago I co-authored, with a marriage counselor, a book called *How To Pick a Mate: The Guide to a Happy Marriage.*)

At any rate, over the years I have come to cherish one trait above all others in girls. And I began learning about this trait from a girl I met when I was twenty-one years old. Her name was Virginia Mathews.

Until I met her I was, in my dating, like a character out of Stendhal seeking a will-o'-the-wisp of the ultimate in feminine desirability (as defined by my college peers). I plotted campaigns to date the best-looking girl or the best dancer or the girl with the highest status within my range and was continually being repulsed or myself repulsing if the winning seemed too easy. I played the role I assumed was expected according to our mores, and the girls played theirs. I encountered dozens of forms of guile, artifice, white lying and outright flimflamming and came to assume that this was all a part of the game.

Then, while still at Penn State, I met Virginia and found that she expected me to like her or not on a completely different basis. And I had to make a rather fast adjustment to stay in her league.

She was a warm, vibrant girl possessing an extraordinary sensitivity to colors and forms. (Today she is a working artist.) By the standards I had been following, however, she was something less than the ultimate in desirability. She was afflicted for most of the first year I knew her with a virulent case of pimples, and she had been earning much of her way through college by making beds in a rooming house and waiting on tables. Yet I was utterly bewitched by her, and mainly because of an outstanding quality I was not used to encountering in girls. She was unvaryingly frank, honest and proud about everything she did and was and wanted to be, and she expected me to be the same. She was trying to be like no

2

one but herself, and she had set high standards for the kinds of behavior she would approve in herself. They mainly concerned integrity.

I frankly was not used to such a candid approach to life and found it, with her, delightfully refreshing. To keep her interested in dating me, my main challenge was to prove that I was not so callow as I seemed. Genuinely puzzled, I asked her how she had learned such candor. She laughed and said that when she was five she had told a fib in order to get a farmer to take her to his farm to help milk the cows. On the way she had fallen out of the car and cut her head. She was certain that God had punished her for telling a lie. "After that," she said, "I was filled with terror every time I even thought of telling a fib."

She also recalled that when she was going through the teen-age craze of collecting autographs, her father, quoting from Shakespeare the advice of Polonius to his son, wrote in her book: "This above all: to thine own self be true!"

I was never able to get even mildly interested in another girl and after four years of courting managed to persuade her to take a chance on marrying me.

We've had a wonderfully varied life, stretching from a period of rather stark unemployment on my part to being televised together with our children on *Person to Person* after *The Status Seekers* appeared. It was Virginia more than anyone else who made me aware of status-seeking tendencies in myself and others.

Through it all she has continued to speak her mind bluntly when she encounters pettiness or scheming or phoniness in others (or in our family). When her gloriously tousled dark brown hair started becoming prematurely gray she refused even to consider dyeing it. (It amuses her that on television she comes across as a striking blonde!) And when our children each reached the age of twelve, she insisted, as a matter of honor, that they pay full fares, though many of their twelve-year-old friends— with parental approval—were not doing so.

Her candor is often the subject of good-natured banter among our friends, as she is apt at parties to blurt out what seems to her to be plain truths. She in turn is amused when reporters interviewing me have noted that I seem unaffected by whatever success I've had as an author. She knows that I wouldn't dare to take on airs and still live with her.

Because of the indoctrination I have received from Virginia over the years, I try to answer all reasonable questions, even when they are hostile, from reporters or people in lecture audiences with complete, good-natured honesty. And I have been delighted to learn how rewarding this is, both in the response from others and in my own feelings about myself.

In my travels during the past year I have found myself talking with at least a dozen women I knew as teen-age girls. Some, I must confess, have not aged very gracefully. What impresses me most is that those who were most conspicuously girls of strong-minded integrity then are the most delightfully stimulating adults today.

Thus it is that I say that the trait I admire most in girls is a stubborn, strong-willed pride in self. Do the very best you can in life, but be glad you are yourself. With that attitude such other crucial things as honesty, integrity and dependability come naturally.

JULIE HARRIS

Promise! What a Lovely Word

Julie Harris holds an unofficial record for versatility in the theater, motion pictures and television. Her stardom was achieved "live" in 1949, when she played a lonely twelve-year-old in The Member of the Wedding. *Unforgettable roles that followed included a fun-loving party girl in* I Am a Camera, *Joan of Arc in* The Lark, *a nun in* Little Moon of Alban *and a deaf-mute in* Johnny Belinda. *Most recently she has been seen on Broadway in the musical comedy* Skyscraper.

When I look at myself in a mirror, I think, what happened to that shy young girl I was when I graduated from high school? Where did I lose her? I remember what she used to dream about—loving and being loved. Why was her head so full of dreams—and not something practical? Well, that shy young girl was given a part in a play, *It's a Gift,* by Curt Goetz, that was to be produced in New York City in March, 1945, at the Playhouse Theater. I guess she had a right to be excited and scared and thoughtful. Not much training behind her, really. Too little. No singing—except once, when she sang *Stormy Weather* in a school play—three summers of acting and dancing lessons at the Perry-Mansfield Theater Camp in Colorado—but no Shakespeare, no long parts committed to memory, no discipline behind her. Well, maybe it was just a beginning. She hoped her voice could be heard at the back of the theater and in the balcony. This was really the beginning, her first experience with the legitimate theater—Broadway! Rehearsals began. They were held in a small, rather dingy room—a rehearsal hall just off Broadway. Chalk marks were put on the floor to indicate where the stage set was, and there were rickety chairs substituting for the stage furniture. The cast assembled. The director talked. And the play began to try to come to life. Oh, how shy that young lady was! She brought a book with her to the rehearsal so that she wouldn't feel lonely if no one talked to her. Why didn't she take a chance? It was taking a big chance to try to act. Why not go all the way? Isn't it better to go out to life with open arms and to say here I am, ready to learn with my heart and mind? If I get knocked down, maybe it *will* hurt, but I can always get up again. I mustn't be cautious. I must be willing to make mistakes, to fall down, to appear foolish, to suffer. Well, that young lady began to suffer—but she was sorry she had to. Not now; she's changed. Julie Harris—that was her name when she was born, December 2, 1925, and it is still her name, except she has added another. It's now Julie Harris Gurian. She is married and has a son. "Oh, think of that," I say to her, "imagine you being so lucky!" But getting back to 1945 and that first job. The young lady was fired on the fifth day of rehearsal; told to go on back to school. I remember not being able to believe it. The management felt I was too inexperienced, and they were right. I agreed with them in my heart, although I never said so out loud. I didn't know how to take direction. I was unskilled. Maybe not untalented. Talent in an actor, I feel, is the desire to become someone else and the joy of showing the character to an audience. I had that but not the skill to bring it out of myself. Now, when I see young people today who are striving to become creative people—teen-agers, as my son admiringly calls the Beautiful People of thirteen to nineteen—I am aware of how much they put into their work, the hours of study and practice, and I wail to myself: Why was I so lazy? I ended up having to work twice as hard, but I accepted that and worked. The theater gave me discipline. I loved to act. I loved the feeling of being part of the cultural impulse of people—that sense of sharing the discovery of ideas put into dramatic form that exists between the audience and the actors. I loved the theater because it made me feel a part of life.

As I said, I was fired from that first play and all my love didn't help me. My heart was full but my brain was empty. So I decided I would have to improve my poor neglected mind. A sudden change—I was rehired two days later and opened in *It's a Gift*. People were kind to me, helped me with my make-up—I didn't know one base from another. I was living with Miss Caroline Hewitt, founder of Miss Hewitt's Classes, a school for girls in New York City. Miss "Hew" adored the theater and had many friends who were professional theater people. Miss Hew was so worried about my lack of technical knowledge that she called Antoinette Perry and asked her what kind of make-up I should use—much to my chagrin. A description of me was given over the telephone, and then the necessary pots and paints were acquired. I had to sing a song in the play—the old tune *I Know Where I'm Going* —and Whitford Kane, a gorgeous actor and a wonderful man, was also acting in the play and he took me aside, taught me the song and we sang it together. I always looked forward to that scene in the play when I ran down a flight of stairs so full of excitement, as the girl I was playing was in love, and I saw Whitford and we had our scene together and sang a song.

Well, that was the beginning for that shy young lady. A dramatic critic from a New York paper even went so far as to say that the young lady showed promise. Promise! What a lovely word. To be young—to be promising. The shy young lady managed to stay in the theater, and in spite of herself, she began to learn, and to learn how much there was to learn, that the learning would never stop. That made everything in life exciting. There is no end to knowledge. The more you know, the more you want to know. As Juliet says to Romeo, "My bounty is as boundless as the sea, my love as deep. The more I give to thee, the more I have, for both are infinite." Gradually my head is catching up with my heart, and one day I may be a whole person. That's nice just to think about. All those days of touring plays—parts that were too much for me—Joan of Arc in *The Lark,* Frankie Addams in *The Member of the Wedding,* Sally Bowles in *I Am a Camera,* Brigit Mary in *Little Moon of Alban,* and the moments before the curtain went up when I felt so helpless before the task. But somehow I had faith enough to stick it out, and each time I did the best I could and each time I knew a little more and could see a little clearer.

But life never seems exactly the same two days in a row. "Boy, oh man, man, oh boy," Frankie's ecstatic cry of release in *The Member of the Wedding,* is still a difficult speech to realize. Just as is Juliet's "Gallop apace, you fiery-footed steeds, towards Phoebus' lodging." But I hope I will always find excitement for the unattainable and try to attain it. For only through trying can I learn, and give my heart and mind a chance to grow. Pierre Auguste Renoir is a great and beautiful painter whose pictures show us the joy of living, and he said on the last day of his life, "I think I am beginning to understand. Today I learned something!"

I guess I didn't lose that young girl after all. She's still part of me. But I hope she's learned something after all this time.

RICHARD GLENN GETTELL

The Age of Discretion

Richard Glenn Gettell, president of Mount Holyoke College since 1957, is an economist whose career has been almost evenly divided among the academic world, business and government service.

An Amherst graduate, he took his doctorate in economics from the University of California and has taught economics at Harvard, Wellesley and Yale. In 1941 he joined the Office of Price Administration, then was transferred to the Air Force as an operations analyst. In 1954 he went to the White House to work on the foreign economic program and as a consultant to the Office of Defense.

I'd like to make a proposal to my own generation and to issue a challenge to all of you in the late teen-age bracket. It is simply this: *Let eighteen be made the age of discretion.*

Throughout history, and in many cultures, a trial by ordeal and a formal initiation have solemnized the. instant when a young person comes of age. It is the moment memorialized in the Bible when one "put away childish things," the occasion when a squire attained knighthood or the time when Hiawatha won his wrestling match with Mondamin. Perhaps the closest parallel in modern times is marked by the ritual exercises of commencement day.

In each instance, after an arduous period of testing (which could result in failure as well as success), an individual could earn relief from adult direction and restraint, be accorded the dignity of being grown up and assume the responsibilities that go along with the new status. Those who failed would continue to be treated as children.

Life is more complicated in modern America. The tests of maturity are more subtle and social values more diverse. A boy or girl who is still supported by parents has not assumed full adult responsibility and cannot claim to be totally independent; the way to maturity is only partially earned. By the same token anyone still engaged in formal education is subject to the strictures of the teacher-pupil or professor-student relationship. Nonetheless the time must come when a young person is given credit for his own successes and, in turn, suffers the penalties of his own failures.

Our own society has many inconsistencies in dealing with this question. Some parents are protective too long, some are permissive too soon. And our laws and customs are confused and confusing; they treat the same individual as a child in some respects and as an adult in others. I believe they should be realigned, and I urge that eighteen could and should be counted the age of discretion, the age when one is given responsibility and when one must assume responsibility. This should be the age when, if one wants to be treated as an adult, one must be prepared to act as an adult.

Why eighteen? It is an arbitrary choice, too early for some, too late for others, but in general not too far off the mark. It is the average age when one enters college, if fortunate enough to be admitted, or when one enters the world after high school. About half of your generation falls in each category.

At this point those who do not go on to college have no choice but to grow up. Many find it a rude shock to be untrained and unwanted; others rise to the challenge and make their way successfully. Boys enter the service or take jobs; girls take jobs or marry. Both are obliged to undertake the responsibilities that fall to members of the adult world. Their childhood is over, whether they like it or not; it is up to them to measure up.

Those who attend college have a wider option. They are postponing their entry into the fully adult world, seeking training that may enable them to enjoy greater success when they do. But they have new freedoms and responsibilities too. Their period of trial is longer. Their capacities are subjected to greater demands. Not all are able to succeed. Some lack the ability, some lack the determination, some stay as juvenile as they were before entering. Others grow up mightily during their college years and eventually provide most of the leadership of the adult world.

If eighteen is a reasonable cutoff point, when one either finishes his schooling and braves the outside world or undertakes the adventure of college, why can't we adapt our legal and social systems accordingly?

I propose that at the age of eighteen young Americans should be counted as adults in each of the following respects. They should be:

1. Eligible for military service. This is true now.

2. Enfranchised as voters. This is currently possible in only a few states, but anyone of an age to serve in the armed forces ought to be given the vote.

3. Legally permitted to drink, but subject to adult penalties for abuse of the privilege.

4. Legally permitted to drive. This would raise the customary age but might keep more of us alive. A modern automobile is an adult toy, not for children.

5. Considered to have reached the age of consent, but prepared to accept the permanent consequences of poor judgment.

6. Given financial responsibility. They should be entitled to borrow or run up bills if prepared to meet them without parental help.

Each of these six points involves duties and obligations to others as well as freedom for yourselves. Adulthood involves penalties for failure and responsibilities which cannot be avoided. Will you be ready to assume them? Are you beginning to prepare yourselves with full understanding of what they will entail?

I think most of you are.

As for the small minority who are not—and they are the unsavory few whose exploits are sensationalized in the news and cause all the noise about teen-age delinquency—I doubt if a few years of aging can add much to their sense of responsibility. Unhappily, there is a minority of adult delinquents in this imperfect world too.

JAN PEERCE

I Was a Teen-age Beatle

Jan Peerce earned his first pay for making music at the age of eleven, singing liturgical music in a synagogue. Since he has come of age, his vocal versatility never ceases to astonish audiences. In this country and abroad, he sings classical and pop with equal ease, ranging from opera and concert hall recitals to radio, TV and films. He was the first American singer to play Moscow's Bolshoi Opera after World War II; he originated the "Culture Corps" plan for sending artists from the United States abroad. Among his many albums are Great Opera Arias *and* Cantorial Masterpieces *(Vanguard);* At Carnegie Hall, Greatest Love Songs *and* Pop Goes Peerce *(United Artists); and* Golden Moments *(RCA Victor).*

I have a confession to make about my youth. Believe it or not, I was a teen-age Beatle. Oh, I didn't have long hair and bangs, of course, and I wasn't clever enough to think up such a catchy name as "The Beatles." But when I was fourteen, I formed a four-piece jazz combo. I played the violin. Different beat and different instruments, true, but remember that in my time, jazz music was regarded in the same light that rock and roll is today. Anyhow, I conceived what I considered a terrific show-biz name for myself—Pinky Pearl. Who knows how my entire life might have changed had I thought to call myself Ringo Starr!

My parents looked askance at my musical ambitions, and I am sure the neighbors were convinced that Pinky Pearl and his motley group were an affront to their ears, a bad influence, and would come to no good. But I was flushed with the heady success of earning a staggering fifty cents a night playing at dances on the Lower East Side. My folks had high hopes that I might become a doctor. They were understandably disappointed when, after a game try, I saw that I was not meant to be the Great Healer. I decided to devote myself to being a violinist. And for more years than I care to remember, it seemed that all I was doing in life was fiddling around!

It was a pretty close race as to whether their disappointment was greater than mine. I just couldn't seem to get a job with a name band. As time went on, I seemed to be standing still while so many others were passing me by. I had no illusions about my voice, either. I was taking singing lessons to help me earn an extra five dollars here and there, warbling at private affairs to stretch my skimpy salary, which by then had to support my wife and family. In fact, there weren't enough engagements to cover the cost of the lessons, but I kept at it anyhow.

It would have been reassuring then had I been able to gaze into a crystal ball and see the strange and exciting turn my life would eventually take and trace the pretty unbelievable odyssey of Pinky Pearl. I certainly could have used the encouragement. Some people are born knowing exactly what they want to do and how to do it. Some are born with the realization that they possess the spark of genius. They are the truly fortunate ones, I guess. But I simply floundered around with the knowledge that as a violinist I wasn't first-rate. For in those stagnant years, I had no way of realizing I was meant for something else. I could not envision that the training, breathing techniques and discipline I was receiving through

14

those constant years of voice lessons—my "sideline"—would some day reap rich dividends and change my life.

There is a certain advantage, I believe, in not having one all-consuming ambition. When you hitch your wagon to only one star, that's all you may ever be able to see ahead of you. Had I been completely devoted to pursuing a career as a violinist, any alternative career would have been unthinkable, any other outlet might have been forgotten. And conversely, I'm glad that I didn't have the desire to be a singer when I was young. For at that time, I simply did not have the wisdom, patience or discipline. Later on, when I grew and matured, things would change and jell. Only in time would the jigsaw puzzle of my life begin to fit into place. And my knowledge of the violin was to be of inestimable musical value when I became a singer.

Actually, had I been concentrating solely on my fiddle, I wouldn't have gotten my first big break—as a tenor at Radio City Music Hall—which eventually led to the Metropolitan Opera, unlikely as it may sound. But I'm getting ahead of the story.

Not putting all my eggs in one basket, I was appearing as both a violinist and a part-time singer with the Astor Hotel Orchestra in New York City. During one particular testimonial dinner, I was belting out a ballad, competing (as usual) with the clanking dinner dishes. Fortunately, there was one person out there who was actually listening to me between the chopped liver and the chicken soup. And fortunately that person happened to be the showman Samuel L. Rothafel, who was then looking for a tenor in a permanent company to be assembled for Radio City Music Hall.

Six years later my roundabout route to the world of classical music would reach culmination as a result of my being heard on the weekly radio show sponsored by the Music Hall.

In November of 1941, I made my debut at the Metropolitan Opera, finally vindicating to my parents (and myself) the specter of Pinky Pearl. True, it wasn't My Son, the Doctor. But My Son, the Opera Singer sounded better than My Son, the Second-Rate Fiddler.

They say that every story should have a point or message, and I am getting to mine. This was not intended to be the standard hearts-and-flowers account of The Struggling Years, nor is it advice to any would-be singer. I wouldn't presume to tell a budding artist to follow my strange road.

You see, I feel that young people today are under the tremendous disadvantage of our present mania for specialization. Teen-agers are expected to know exactly what they want to do in life—whether they will go into accounting, engineering, nursing, teaching—exactly what their college majors will be, and after college, where they should set their sights. Well, as I said before, there are some who know and always have known exactly what they want, and they will get there. But most of us may not be sure we are aiming right; even if we hit the bull's-eye—is that what we really wanted? That's why it's so important to be flexible and to try to develop a number of interests, whether you use them for a cushion or a steppingstone. History books are full of people who stumbled onto the right path by sheer accident. And sometimes the best way to find your ultimate destination is simply to change your course.

I'm not saying anyone should sit around and just wait for things to happen. And I don't believe in changing your mind every other day. Find some sort of goal and, like any goal, try to achieve it. But have the courage to change it if you have to.

I guess what I'm trying to say is simply this: Hitch your wagon to a star—but every now and then, keep looking around out of the corner of your eye.

KENNETH TYNAN

The Most Invaluable Freedom of Them All

Kenneth Tynan wrote his first drama criticism at sixteen and has since etched a reputation as the brightest, most stinging theater critic to enliven the English scene since the days of George Bernard Shaw. A collection of his reviews from 1950 to 1960 has been published under the title Curtains. *He is currently the literary manager of England's government-sponsored National Theatre. He has one daughter, Tracy, who is in her teens.*

Are you planning to go to college? If so, here's a word or two about what it certainly *won't* be like; and it's up to you to decide whether my experiences at an English university leave you envious, appalled or plain unmoved. I went to Oxford straight from high school a couple of months after the end of World War II. I had won a scholarship, by dint of careful work and careful bluff, and overnight I was transported from a provincial suburb to a citadel of privilege. It was a real change of life, quite unlike what a young American feels when he goes to Harvard or Yale. For one thing, higher education is open to a much larger percentage of Americans than of Englishmen. For another, Oxford and Cambridge get the cream of the crop—the best teachers and the brightest pupils—in a way that Harvard and Yale never did. Our senior universities were both founded in the Middle Ages, and they rapidly established a stranglehold on English culture. So great was their power that London, the capital city, saw no need to have a university of its own until well into the nineteenth century. A steady stream of writers, politicians, philosophers and scientists has poured out of these two market towns—known collectively as "Oxbridge"—to govern England, to mold its opinions and to create its mental climate. And if a genius happens to emerge from some other source (as Shakespeare did, among many others), Oxford and Cambridge know how to handle the situation: they tell England what to think of him. Going to "Oxbridge" is like joining an ancient club, and although the membership is less exclusive than it was twenty years ago, about half the undergraduates still come from the expensive private academies that the English mysteriously call "public schools."

Oxford is what you make of it; most of your time's your own, to use or squander, as you see fit. From a world of school timetables and nightly homework, I walked into an atmosphere of terrifying freedom. My subject was English literature, which meant that for three years I would read nothing else. (At Oxford you cannot take more than one course at a time.) A tutor was assigned to me—a brilliant critic and moralist named C. S. Lewis, who explained that it wasn't compulsory for me to go to lectures. All I had to do was write one essay a week and spend an hour listening to his comments on it. Otherwise, I was on my own. I ought to add that if I had been a girl, things would have been tougher; women were not admitted to Oxford until the end of the last century, and they are still regarded as alien intruders who have to justify their presence by working like slaves. They live in ugly red-brick colleges, cut off from the male part of the university, and I can't imagine what attracts them to the place, unless perhaps it's the fact that at Oxford there are five men to every girl. I have said that I walked into freedom: I also walked into history—and upper-class history at that.

There's a gulf between Pittsburgh and Harvard, but it's the merest ditch compared with the gulf between Birmingham, my home town, and Magdalen College, Oxford. The room beneath mine had been occupied by Oscar Wilde; the Duke of Windsor had spent his college days in a nearby cloister, and so, two centuries before, had Edward Gibbon, the great historian of the Roman Empire. And here was I, who had never owned a dinner jacket, never shot a pheasant, and never even eaten an oyster. The past was all around me, even in my work; at that time, the English literature course at Oxford included nothing written after 1830, although it forced you to learn a barbarous, extinct dialect called Anglo-Saxon.

I felt out of my depth in every way, and I reacted by splashing out in all directions. To coin a phrase, I woke up to my irresponsibilities. Though I couldn't join the ruling class, I could lick it. I acted in plays and directed them, and these undergraduate efforts were reviewed by the London drama critics, who would have ignored me if I had gone to a provincial university. I talked my head off at the Oxford Union, the most famous debating club in Britain, where Cabinet ministers and similar celebrities appear as guest speakers every week; and I contributed to a dozen university magazines, with results that led a London publisher to commission my first book. I bumped into Dylan Thomas and Truman Capote; I also met Mae West, whom I invited to a party held on Sexagesima Sunday, and Princess (now Queen) Elizabeth, whose visit to Oxford was marked by a specially composed masque in which I played the lead. I bought a suit of purple doeskin and a golden satin shirt, in which garb I was burned in effigy by a crowd of roaring athletes.

And I discovered the charms of talk. In my first year at Oxford there were floods of it, during which one did nothing—one didn't even drink; one smoked instead, getting drier and more emotionally parched, and feeling the first twinges of guilt. The wish and the power to work, to write, to achieve, seemed to wither away as one talked through so many nights, from dusk to dawn. Between chats of this kind (which were actually very fruitful) I gave parties in barns, on river steamers and in church belfries; and once, in 1948, I was arrested and fined because—according to the indictment—I "did fire a certain firework in a certain street, contrary to Section 80 of the Explosives Act, 1875." I fell in and out of love like a moth with two dozen flames, to one of whom I publicly said: "Any altar I might lead you to would be purely sacrificial." I was tall, skinny and unkempt, a state which moved a friend of mine to describe me as a final proof of the scientific hypothesis that the hair and nails of a corpse continue to grow for several weeks after death. Meanwhile, I trumpeted slogans like: "This has been called the age of the Little Man—it is really the age of the Dwarf." In short, I was outrageous and almost unbearable. You might easily have loathed me.

But the point is that I was free to be unbearable. I had three years in which to experiment with any kind of eccentricity that appealed to me, and in which to learn—from the men and boys around me—how far I could go. Most people wait until they are grown up to spread their wings; by then it is often too late for them to learn how to do so without injuring others. Oxford teaches you the accepted limits of civilized freedom. The limits are sometimes too civilized, too politely upper-class, and this I deplore; but the freedom is genuine and irreplaceable. For anyone young, it is the first and most invaluable freedom of all. Sir Max Beerbohm, the great essayist, once said about English youth: "The nonsense which was knocked out of them at school is all put gently back at Oxford or Cambridge." Which is just as it should be. Nonsense is part of our birthright; and the more we are allowed to indulge in it—the more we are encouraged to make our own mistakes—the healthier we grow up to be. An error in good faith is worth fifty copied truths.

RICHARD RODGERS

How To Get a Start in the Theater

Richard Rodgers has enriched the musical theater for more than forty years. He wrote his first song at fourteen, collaborated first with Lorenz Hart, then Oscar Hammerstein II, to write forty-eight musicals for stage, night clubs, television and films. Oklahoma!, Carousel, South Pacific, The King and I *and* The Sound of Music *are among the most memorable. He has two daughters, both of whom work in the theater.*

A pretty young girl writes me every day from an American small town, often enclosing her picture. Each day it's a different girl and a different postmark, but the letter is the same.

"Dear Mr. Rodgers," it begins, and the next sentence is always: "How can I get a start in the theater? I've been singing since I was six, and people here tell me that I have a good voice and should be on the stage. Could you advise me as to what I should do?"

I see this girl often. Years may pass after she has written the letter, perhaps, but one day she walks across a stage in one of the auditions we hold regularly. She smiles hesitantly, and sometimes she says, "I'm a little nervous today."

She doesn't have to tell me. I can see her hands shake

and I would have detected those first telltale, trembling notes when she started to sing. But I'm glad she did tell me. It helps her to voice her nervousness and it gives me an excuse to use the bagful of bad jokes I keep for such occasions. At least if she knows that I know she's nervous, she may relax a little more, feeling I might make allowances for that.

And I do. After all, my two daughters, Mary and Linda, have chosen a career in the theater. Not singing, though. Both of them compose music, following in my footsteps, and I couldn't be more pleased. And I hope some producer will always hear their songs to the last note.

We've always had a policy in our office to hear a singer through. It's like letting a man finish a sentence—common courtesy. Most people at an audition sing only one chorus anyway. Then they look at you pleadingly and stop, hoping you will say, "Could I hear you sing something else?" In any event, we listen to all thirty-two bars of one song. We believe in encouraging young talent as much as we can. After all, we are in the business of trying to get work for young people and to help the theater in general. Sometimes the sounds at these auditions are painful, and you have to put up with them.

So I write back to my beautiful young correspondent and say:

Your first concern must be the basic equipment. You should study singing—in New York, Los Angeles or San Francisco, preferably, where good teachers live and work. But if that isn't possible, then in your home town. Every small town has a competent voice teacher, or there's one nearby. Shirley Jones commuted thirty miles from her home town of Smithton, Pennsylvania, to Pittsburgh for singing lessons; and it was her voice teacher who brought her to our attention. So this unknown girl got to play Laurey in the movie version of *Oklahoma!* and went on to win an Academy Award in *Elmer Gantry.* Then put that study to work. I don't care if it's a high school auditorium, a church social or an amateur theatrical production, get out there and sing! An aspiring singer has to establish contact with an audience and find out what that consists of and what it demands from her. Every appearance you make will help to polish your good points and to smooth out the rough spots and shortcomings. This is the greatest training in the world, and there is no substitute for it.

See as much theater, especially the musicals, as you can. By critically studying other performers' techniques, poise and presence, you will be able to avoid some of their pitfalls and perhaps adapt some of their good points to your own personality.

Don't try for the professional theater without careful preparation. Once you've faced enough audiences, as a young singer, you will be ready to compete against professional talents for jobs. But the worst thing you can do is to come to New York—or any big city—unprepared professionally and unsupported financially. Teachers and audiences (even church congregations) will tell you when you're ready professionally, if you have doubts yourself. But the financial side is equally important. Work at a job and save money, borrow it from parents or inquire about scholarships—but have some assured income for at least the first year. Because while you're in New York, it's important to keep studying. People have the mistaken notion that singers in Broadway shows have all day free to sleep until noon and roam around shopping until show time. The exact opposite is true. Most youngsters in the theater today fill their nonperforming hours with lessons of every kind, from music and voice projection and acting to dancing and fencing and languages.

And finally, follow every lead, so that you can be seen and heard by Broadway producers. Attend auditions, prepared with music. Mingle with other singers to learn who's casting what and what producers are seeing people. It's very easy, for example, to get an audition with the Rodgers and Hammerstein office. You simply contact the office in New York by mail or telephone and ask for an interview. You'll be seen and heard by someone competent—not immediately by me. One of my staff will hear you sing; this would be in the nature of a screening.

And at some point, I will be shown the result of this screening. If it coincides with a production in which we are immediately involved, another appointment will be made for you to sing before more people. If not, the information will be filed and cross-indexed. The notations on the file cards go like this: "Replacement possibility for youngster in *The Sound of Music*" or "Could be good Julie in *Carousel*." More than four thousand cards are in our files, and they are often consulted by other producers.

"We're casting a musical and need a young blonde about seventeen or eighteen who has a lyric soprano. Could you recommend someone?" they'll call and ask. (I wouldn't doubt that if they said, "We need a baritone with three arms," my staff could find one in the file cards.) We're glad to suggest several candidates to them. Hoarding young talent is the last thing we want to do.

And through these auditions and screenings, young people like Shirley Jones, Florence Henderson, Sal Mineo, Barbara Luna and Patrick Adiarte have gotten their first important breaks in Rodgers and Hammerstein musicals. We gave Florence Henderson her first solo lines in *South Pacific* and later recommended her for the stage musical *Fanny*. Sal Mineo and Patrick Adiarte appeared as the young Prince in *The King and I;* Barbara Luna started in show business as one of Ezio Pinza's children in *South Pacific*.

We keep tabs on new talent because we are constantly casting road companies or revivals of our shows. For instance, in one week this past summer, there were *sixty-one* productions of *Oklahoma!* playing across the United States.

I can't deny that it was no accident that both my daughters wanted to work in the theater. I exposed my daughters to both theater and music from the time they could walk and talk.

When Mary was four, I took her to see her first Broadway musical, *Jumbo*. (After all, if your father writes *Jumbo*, you should certainly see it, especially if it is full of animals and clowns, Jimmy Durante—and your father's music.) Linda cut *her* teeth at four on *Too Many Girls*, also one of my musicals.

The first piece Mary learned on the piano was one of my songs, *Why Can't I?* from *Spring Is Here*. We used to play it as a duet. And Linda read music before she could read English. When you think about it, music is less complicated than English, and more dependable. The note on the second line of a staff is always G in music—but in English the letter G can be pronounced soft or hard or not at all.

I began playing a musical game called "Intervals" with my girls when they were tots. I would seat them near the piano, out of sight of my fingers, and then I would strike two notes, like C and G. They would have to tell me the interval, or distance, between these two notes: was it a third, fourth or fifth? (It was a fifth.) This was great ear training for them, and they grew to be very acute musically. The game got to be exciting because the girls would race to answer first, and I think I enjoyed it as much as they did.

Later, when I was thirty-nine, I started taking piano lessons again, and then Linda and Mary had to fight for the piano because the Old Man had it. This had an interesting and subtle psychological effect on their interest in the piano and music. Little girls are always in love with their fathers (something I never discouraged) and want to do what he does. And the more the piano was hard to get, the more they wanted to get at it and practice as I did.

The girls also went to the children's concerts in New York, to hear the music of the great composers. Today they write for these concerts. Mary, for example, has written scripts for Leonard Bernstein's successful television series of music for young people. She also wrote the music for the Broadway musical *Once upon a Mattress* and the TV musical *Feathertop*. Linda composed the music for a revue for children called *Three To Make Music,* for which Mary provided the lyrics. Mary Martin used these songs in a special television program for children, with excellent reception from the youngsters. Linda also wrote the music for a Golden Records album called *A Child's Introduction to Jazz,* for which Marshall Barer and Mary Rodgers wrote the lyrics.

Having all these composers in the family has had a curious effect on my grandchildren. They think anyone who comes to the house and doesn't write music is peculiar. Once, after a guest told Mary's son Richard, aged nine, that he designed buildings for a living, Richard turned to us and asked, "What's wrong with *him?*"

I never offer criticism of the things my daughters have written. I want them to stand on their own feet as much as possible. Besides, children don't take very well to parental criticism about anything, from make-up to music. That old saying, "It's more blessed to give than to receive," just doesn't apply to advice from parents.

Mary had to face the possibility that people might say I wrote her songs, or that she had cribbed her style from me. I think she faced it well, and I was pleased when critics judged her work on its own merits in reviewing *Once upon a Mattress.* In essence, they said, "This girl doesn't need her father. She has her own talent." And she has.

So because I know what struggles young people face in trying to get a toehold in the theater, I always answer my young correspondent who wants to become a singer, and give as much advice as I can. I suggest that if it's possible, she try to study at an institution like the Juilliard School of Music in New York. Their high level of voice training has my respect. Perhaps only twice in an audition of twenty people will I think enough of the voice to ask, "Where did you study?" Almost invariably, the answer has been "Juilliard."

I would probably ask this young girl one final question: "Do you want a singing career *enough?*" Because a career in show business demands many difficult sacrifices before success can be won, and she must be prepared for that. But if her answer is "Yes," then my advice would be to concentrate on her goal, as Oscar Hammerstein II wrote in one of his beautiful lyrics to my music, "with hope in your heart, and you'll never walk alone."

S. J. PERELMAN

Do Anything Else, but Lay Off the Quill

S. J. Perelman describes himself as "button-cute, rapier-keen, wafer-thin and pauper-poor . . . whose tall, stooping figure is better known to the twilight half-world of five continents than to Publishers' Row." He has been keeping readers up past their bedtime since 1925, when his first book, Dawn Ginsbergh's Revenge, *was published. He has written stage plays—most recently* The Beauty Part—*screenplays for the Marx Brothers, TV scripts and books, the most recent being* The Rising Gorge.

I hope you don't mind if I brush away a tear or two; this is something of a sentimental occasion for me, a rhinestone jubilee, you might say. It's exactly forty-five years since I first found myself—in the vertical position then—dehydrating before an audience of my peers. I was at that time a student in the Classical High School in Providence, Rhode Island, and I played a supporting role in a remarkable pageant entitled *Pocahontas, Get Your Gun.* It was a performance that is still spoken of in whispers wherever actors congregate. I was a strikingly impressive figure in my red flannels, with a goose feather braided through my topknot, and I thought that I crept into every heart. Unfortunately that other distinguished Thespian, Lionel Barrymore, was also appearing at the time, in a play called *The Copperhead* at the Providence Opera House, and he bribed the local drama critics to ignore me. I never forgave the man; years later, when we met face to face on the back lot at M-G-M—or back to back on the front lot, I don't remember which—I looked right through him, cut him cold. You can get pretty vindictive when you're an Indian as a boy.

I made a second sterling appearance that same winter; I was the youngest, and it goes without saying, the most brilliant member of my school debating team. We were pitted against the Allegra Pellagra High School of Hookworm, N. C., on the three-fold proposition "Resolved, that the pen is mightier than the sword, that football is a brutal sport, and that the Philippines should be given their independence." Being classical students, my colleagues and I were dressed in long purple togas, we had bay and laurel wreaths looped across our foreheads and we carried clay tablets—all of which contrasted rather oddly with my short corduroy knickerbockers. The contest was nip and tuck all the way, and at times the audience, rocked in the rhythmic sway of oratory, turned pale with what could have been either excitement or *mal de mer*. Nonetheless, I was assured later that my eloquence was such that I could empty any auditorium in the world in two minutes flat. I thought that was the nicest thing anyone said to me that evening; it certainly was the cleanest. Now that we've recaptured the past in a fashion calculated to curl the toes of Marcel Proust, we can get down to the business at hand. My vocation, it may have leaked out to you, is that of a writer, which means that I sit in a hot little room stringing words together like beads at so many cents per bead. It's shabby-genteel work and, on the whole, poorly paid, but I'm too fragile to drive a brewery truck and I'm too nervous to steal. Now, for some reason I've never been able to fathom, many young people are fascinated by the lives that writers lead; they think it's romantic. It's about as romantic as working for the United States Post Office and, in fact, it has a great deal in common with it. You handle a vast quantity of paper and envelopes and stamps, and you handle it twice—once when you send your manuscripts out to the magazines, and a second time—but I see you've already beat me to it. The chief drawback of the literary life as I practice it is that you smoke an inordinate amount of tobacco and that you live in a constant state of fantasy, which any headshrinker will tell you is very bad for the pysche. It being the only game in town, however, I stick with it doggedly, forever hoping that my ticket in the Irish Hospital Sweepstakes will pay off or that some wealthy sheepherding uncle in Australia will cool and leave me his bundle. In the poolrooms I frequent, it has often reached my ears that the chief advantage of being a writer is that it allows you to sleep late in the morning. Don't believe it. You can enjoy the same privilege as a night counterman in a cafeteria, and, what's more, in that job you can always bring home stale Danish pastries for the kiddies.

Sad to say, no matter how earnestly I counsel anyone against the rigors and uncertainty of a writer's existence, there is always in every assemblage one boy or girl with a deeply serious mien and a forehead like a Burpee cantaloupe who refuses to be deterred. He or she has seen photographs of Arthur Miller and Mary McCarthy, their profiles nobly silhouetted against the sky and decorated with breathless captions about the scads of money their works have earned. How enthralling it would be, the fledgling murmurs, to consort with such glamour pusses, to listen to their pithy comments on politics and the arts, to roister with them in the bohemian locales they frequent! Well, it is quite possible that some writers lead rich and turbulent lives lunching at Twenty-One, consuming double Gibsons at one literary cocktail party after another and dancing the night away in Harlem. I personally have never encountered these distractions. The last time I saw Arthur Miller, his legs were twined around a stool in a Third Avenue hamburger joint and he was staring moodily into an empty coffee mug. Judging from the crossword puzzle propped against the sugar bowl, he was engaged in intellectual labor so profound that it would have been sacrilege to disturb him, and I forebore. Mary McCarthy I also saw in midtown New York—not, as one might suppose, emerging from Mainbocher's' salon or the Four Seasons, but hovering over a display of citrus in a cut-rate supermart. She was methodically palpating half a dozen grapefruit to discover a ripe one, and her frustration was clearly at fever heat, for she was panting audibly and seemed on the verge of an apoplectic seizure.

But hold on, you object—granting that playwrights and novelists may lead humdrum lives, it must be sparkling fun as well as stupendously enriching to write for movies and television. If your geography permits you to spend ten minutes at the confluence of Hollywood Boulevard and Vine Street in the motion-picture citadel, you will perceive the answer in an eyeblink. That picturesque scarecrow in rags who just shuffled by is a former screen writer, forcibly retired because the movie industry as such has ceased to exist. Here comes the man who supplanted him, an author of TV scripts. He appears to be solvent, forceful, organized, does he not? Why then does he twitch in that extraordinary fashion? And how on earth did he get all those curious facial tics? Well, my dears, those are souvenirs, minor afflictions that result from his livelihood. Any opinions he has are strictly accidental; his head, as you will observe, bobbles in a 360-degree arc like a Christmas tiger's so that he can agree with anyone, however lunatic. He has just rewritten, for the thirteenth time, a script commissioned by a major network, and he is hastening into that drugstore opposite for ten cents' worth of cyanide of potassium to end it all.

Well, it's been simply wizard chatting with you, and if there's anything further I can do to dissuade you from the writing game, like burning down a typewriter factory or manacling you to your copy of Xenophon's *Anabasis*, 32 do feel free to call on me. I'm only sorry we didn't meet forty-five years ago, when you could have seen me in my prime in *Pocahontas, Get Your Gun*. Perhaps, if you're sufficiently curious about it, you might contact some knowledgeable person in Washington—say, at the Bureau of Indian Affairs. Speaking of which, I once knew an Iroquois girl near Canandaigua, New York—but that's quite another story.

SHELLEY WINTERS

The Loneliest Years of My Life

Shelley Winters, winner of both an Academy Award and an Emmy, decided as a teen-ager that she wanted to be an actress. In the years since, she has undergone a metamorphosis from dizzy blonde to serious stage and film actress. She is still well remembered on Broadway for her performance in A Hatful of Rain. *In films, she won Academy Award nominations for* A Double Life *and* A Place in the Sun *and finally won her first Oscar with* The Diary of Anne Frank, *her second for* A Patch of Blue. *Her career has also included live television shows, one of which won her the Emmy Award.*

When the editor of *SEVENTEEN* asked me to write an article, I was somewhat reluctant to do so for two reasons. The first being, I remember the period of sixteen to twenty as the most painful and, in a way, the loneliest years of my life. The second: I realize that some of the feelings about myself that I acquired during those years have stuck with me during my adult life.

I don't know how other "adults" feel inside but, although I look much different now, I guess I still somehow feel very "teen-ageish" and like to be around people of this age. They teach me much and, in a sense, they keep me young because their opinions are quite accurate on where the world is going.

In a way, the war years and the postwar years were much simpler times to grow up in. The issues were much simpler than they are now. They were something to think about, to fight for. And, in a way, they were easier to understand. I still think there is something to fight for, but it is hard to know it clearly as there are now constantly new and shifting things in both our moral and political life, and the family-life unit is much less stable. But I will tell you about my feelings and then tell you what I have observed from teen-agers—whom I feel very close to, since I teach acting classes and get a chance to meet the kids in all parts of the country when I tour in summer stock.

All my friends and I knew very clearly what we wanted to be and do, often to our own detriment. We drove toward our goals so hard. I never finished high school because I quit to attend dramatic school at night and model in the daytime. To this day I am sorry for it. And although through reading and extension college classes I have gotten some formal education, I still feel inadequate on some deep level when I am with people who have had college educations and whom I would like to know better. Perhaps the disparity in our educational levels is not so great as I think, but the feelings I acquired when I left high school are still there. So, although I am no longer the blonde bombshell of my early career, I often find myself acting that part because I feel I won't be accepted as an intelligent, educated woman. These feelings limit my social world considerably. The discipline of study, of developing your mind so that it *wants* to study and likes to and considers it fun, which I have seen in many young people, I have never acquired. These feelings of inadequacy have made me make life decisions which have proved to be terribly serious mistakes. In my field, the theater, an actor, I believe, can portray most truthfully what he knows. And his spectrum of emotions and characters is deeply limited by his education and experience. In other words, I am saying, "A smart actress can play a dumb one but I don't think a dumb actress can play a smart one." I am quite sure this applies to many other professions as well.

One of the most tragic examples I ever saw of this feeling of inadequacy was in James Dean. I first met Jimmy at the Actors' Studio in New York. Then I got to know him quite well in Hollywood at Warner Brothers, where I was shooting a film with Jack Palance called *I Died a Thousand Times*. Jimmy was shooting *Giant* with George Stevens, the director who discovered me.

Jimmy was a beautiful young man, extremely talented, but his opinion of himself and the feelings of unworthwhileness made him value himself and his life very lightly. If he asked a question or wanted and needed the attention of someone who was preoccupied, as his director was, with many problems, Jimmy immediately assumed that he was being rejected, not realizing that the person was busy and could not gratify his request at once. He covered all these feelings with a cool manner, but he didn't have enough in his education and background to allow him to handle success and the disappointments that go with success at such an early age. He had a marvelous sense of humor and so it was very difficult to tell just how deeply hurt he was for the slightest reason, unless you knew him very well. He was highly intelligent, but I am not talking about intelligence. I am talking about academic knowledge, which gives you methods and alternatives in handling what happens to you in the world. There is an incident that stands out most vividly in my mind about Jimmy. A bunch of us had gone to see a preview of *On the Waterfront* at Columbia and we were coming up Sunset Boulevard after the show. I was in a car with a young man and Jimmy kept circling us in his Porsche (the car he was killed in). He was acting as if it were a game, and I guess I knew even then that his idea of fun was covering up a terrible loneliness and intolerable dissatisfaction with the world and himself.

Most people think of making movies as a marvelous

profession, but a performance is only really good when the actor has exposed some deep level of himself. That is when an audience becomes involved with the movie. It is hard to explain, but suppose you had a tic and you had trained yourself not to show this to the world and you were involved in a profession in which you knew you could only be effective if you abandoned your covering-up mechanism and allowed the world to see your tic. That is perhaps a superficial analogy, but it is the only thing I can think of to explain to a non-actor what an actor has to go through.

Jimmy Dean was born with that talent and studied and developed it, and so he was constantly having to use in his work the things he really wanted to hide from the world. I think if he had been lucky enough to have a teacher or friend who could have taught him to tolerate the anxiety his work generated, he would, perhaps, still be alive. I have never talked about him before, but because I read so much now about dropouts in high school, I think he would want me to. Something in the torment of his youth made the young of all countries and languages identify and respond to him, and they still do.

The world is and can be a beautiful place and we can help make it more beautiful for everyone, but we have to be alive and functioning and mature to do so. The first way to do it, I believe, is to acquire as much as possible of the human knowledge that mankind has been able to accumulate for us. In other words, get as much schooling as possible.

I once worked in a play by Tennessee Williams called *The Night of the Iguana*. The play is about loneliness and the needs that human beings have for a feeling of "completion." Not just sexual completion, which is an easy explanation, but of the need for human companionship of the opposite sex that will make the world more complete. Tennessee Williams is a powerful writer and every night I tried to make the part fresh and new. I did this in different scenes by remembering parallel things that I had seen or read, and I knew, in some secret part of my heart, that even though I was playing a simple woman, I could have fulfilled this role better if I had finished senior-year English literature and developed the inside of my head instead of just bleaching the outside.

My life has taught me that if you are able to attain fully what it is that you want to achieve, that is the closest thing to happiness.

JOHN KNOWLES

All Split Up

John Knowles was born in West Virginia and began writing at the age of twelve. His first professionally published story was A Turn with the Sun, *which appeared when he was twenty-three. After he had worked as a reporter and editor for six years, his first novel,* A Separate Peace, *was published in 1960. It has become a favorite with young people; a stage version is now being prepared by Edward Albee. Mr. Knowles based his second novel,* Morning in Antibes, *on a period spent in the south of France, and his only work of nonfiction,* Double Vision: American Thoughts Abroad, *on a trip through the Middle East and the Greek islands. His most recent novel is* Indian Summer.

I'm getting a little tired of the emphasis on youth. Is anybody else?

I'm also tired of the emphasis on "senior citizens" and "young marrieds" and the "prime of life" group. I think it's a shame that the American people are being more and more rigidly divided horizontally, isolating all the twelve-year-olds together, and all the seventeen-year-olds, and all the fortyish people, and all the sixty-plus group and so on. I don't think this exists anywhere else in the world, nor has it ever existed before in history.

I saw that clearly when I visited the past not long ago. I found the past in a desert in the Middle East, between Egypt and Arabia. There, roaming through the wastes from oasis to oasis were the Arab tribes known as the Bedouin, still leading the nomadic lives our distant ancestors led. Among them a young man of seventeen, for example, would live and work and play with his uncles and his cousins and his eight-year-old niece and nephew, continually and probably unconsciously absorbing knowledge of life from his elders and communicating it to his juniors. And I lived for a while on a Greek island and in an Italian village and in a French town and on an Irish farm, and always there was this intermingling of the old and the middle-aged and the young and the children, a natural interchange of learning and acting and developing.

But we don't have that any more in America. It seems that a twenty-three-year-old hasn't a word to say to someone eighteen, and as for an attempt by someone forty to speak to someone twenty-three. . . ! In lock step each age group clomps ahead together, the blind marching with the blind, all of them knowledgeable and ignorant in the same degree, unwilling and unable to absorb knowledge from those who have gone ahead, unwilling and unable to pass it to those behind, who are completely unprepared to accept it anyway. It's pathetic, this isolation by age, and I wish I knew who was at fault. Preoccupied elders and arrogant youth exist, but so do older people eager to get to know the young, and vice versa.

I have been lucky in this myself. My particular way of life and my interests have brought me close to people of all ages. There was, however, a period a few years ago when everyone I knew intimately seemed for some reason to be about fifty years old. And did they *have* to go home so early at night, I eventually began asking myself in exasperation. It's true I was learning a lot about behavior and the ways of the world and painting and foreign countries through these friendships, but *why* didn't they like to skin dive?

Then I moved to another city and said to myself, "I want all my friends to be twenty-five or younger." And to a large extent I succeeded in gathering these people ten years or so younger than myself around me. It was exhilarating to know so much more than they did, to have them sometimes hang on my words because of what I could tell them from my, to them, vast store of experience. But eventually what they said to me began to pall a little. Broken young hearts and groping ambition and impulsive mistakes were such old stories by now to me. And weren't they restive now and then because I was too sedate, too settled, for them?

I moved again, which is very helpful in these experiments in finding friends. This time I tried to have some friends who were a good deal older and others considerably younger than myself. And, as always, I had certain friends who were my own age, with whom I shared the peculiar sense of interlocked destinies that exact contemporaries have.

In this way I've tried to re-create in our artificial American society the natural conditions of the past. I think everybody should try. Of course, as a writer, it's easier for me to do this than if I were in many other fields; a writer is automatically thought of as a maverick, offbeat, out of step because of his profession. Perhaps I am out of step, having dinner one night with a married couple in their late fifties who can tell me about American theater in the 1920's, friends who are able to criticize something about the way I act or talk or deal with people without arousing too much resentment in me. I can accept these criticisms from them as I don't think I would be able to do from people my own age or younger. And the next night I may go to a gathering of people in their twenties, and there the new motions in music and dancing and thoughts and hopes and cars and exercises and plans— from the Peace Corps to the Monkey—surround me.

I'm happy only when my life has this kind of combination. Perhaps I am out of step; I pity everybody who isn't.

ARTUR RUBINSTEIN

Make No Conditions

Artur Rubinstein, born in Warsaw, Poland, made his debut in the United States in 1906, at the age of seventeen. He has since become the most celebrated of living pianists, touring millions of miles to play the piano both here and abroad. Recording for RCA Victor, Rubinstein has sixty-six albums currently in print. Among them are his interpretations of Chopin (Ballades, Mazurkas, Nocturnes, Polonaises, Waltzes *and* Piano Concertos No. 1 and 2), *the* Five Piano Concertos of Beethoven *and* Piano Music of Liszt and Grieg.

People are always surprised that in spite of my age I seem so young, that I am still playing the piano and giving concerts, that I have a lot of vitality. It does not seem surprising to me. I simply feel that way, that's all.

I live by one principle: Enjoy life with no conditions! People say, "If I had your health, if I had your money, oh, I would enjoy myself." It is not true. I would be happy if I were lying sick in a hospital bed. It must come from the inside. That is the one thing I hope I have contributed to my children, by example and by talk: to make no conditions, to understand that life is a wonderful thing and to enjoy it, every day, to the full.

The majority of people feel they must be doing something all the time. Many who sit all day in an office or clean the house or work in a factory think that if they sit down at a sidewalk café and fold their arms and look at people, they are merely wasting time. They are wrong. In watching people and enjoying life, they may only then be truly alive.

If I were a historian and were to put headings on various periods of history, I would call this the age of frustration. Look around at our world: skyscrapers, radar, atomic energy. In my own lifetime I have seen the coming of the automobile, the airplane, the phonograph, so many things. When I was a boy, there were the ships, the railways and the horse-drawn carriage; that was all.

But what use have men made of all this? We are animals, true, but we are worse than the dog, the rat, the lion. If a lion is sated, he will not bother you unless he is attacked. Most beasts are this way. Who but man has put so many to death, more in this century than in our entire history? Millions of young people slaughtered, old people, children. We are all responsible—I mean all humanity—for allowing the world to become this way. Who can blame young people for snapping their fingers in the face of an older generation which has brought them to war and slaughter twice in a living man's memory?

To me the world is divided into two kinds of people: those who are conscious and those who are unconscious. To me there is no difference among men when it comes to their color, their race, their religion; they are all equal. Only the degree of their awareness of the world they live in, of the joy and the pleasure of living, of the need of sharing that awareness with others and bringing it to their fellow men (if they happen to be fortunate enough to have talent) is a measure of this difference.

During my long life I have learned one lesson: that the most important thing is to realize *why* one is alive—and I think it is not only to build bridges or tall buildings or

46

make money, but to do something truly important, to do something for humanity. To bring joy, hope, to make life richer for the spirit because you have been alive, that is the most important thing.

Music is like none of the other arts. For a long time, I didn't understand what music really meant; then I read Nietzsche, the German philosopher who explained that all art is divided into two types, the Apollonian, which comes from the intellect, and the Dionysian, which is pure emotion—and the latter is music (no matter what some modern composers say to the contrary). An actor is bound to the meaning of the word; a painter shows you what he thinks of another object; but an interpreter of music can give you his unique presentation of the music. It does not exist without him. A score is only notes on paper; how many men can read one? Take it into the jungle, who will understand? Yet music and dance were the earliest rituals known to man in every culture.

I may sit down at the piano and perform a sonata in the spirit of hope, another may sit down and play the same score in a state of melancholy, a third musician may be flippant. Each is right in his own approach, and each offers a distinct experience.

In order to pass it on, an interpreter must experience the emotion himself. I must feel everything in my own fingers before I can hold the audience in my grasp. It is a kind of magnetism, almost hypnotic. Paderewski was able to seize an audience completely, although technically he played the piano poorly; you can hear that on his records. But he was able to mesmerize people in performance. When you give a concert, if there is no spark in you, the audience feels nothing.

Years ago, I noticed mostly middle-aged people at my concerts; whether it was because they had more money or what, I don't know, but now there are always hundreds of young people—teen-agers, boys and girls—in my audiences. I play many college recitals; there are always enthusiastic young people who come to talk with me about music.

Statistically speaking, more women than men seem to enjoy music, perhaps because they are able to express emotion directly. In our culture, girls are allowed to cry, to laugh without inhibition; they don't worry about the impression they present to the world. With men, it is different. We men cannot cry. We are taught never to let ourselves be seen with tears in our eyes. For us it isn't so easy to accept the experience of music. But this is changing. In fact, touring over the years, I find that different countries have become more interested in music as they have diminished in power, politically or economically. Music becomes an expression of mood; it allows them to express themselves emotionally.

In my family, I am the extroverted one. I have always been that way. I make friends easily. My wife is not so open and outgoing until she knows someone well. Of my four children (they came in "pairs," about ten years apart) two are like me; the other two resemble their mother. Fortunately, however, all of them are interested in life. I am glad of that, for we have brought up our children with trust and faith. They have been allowed much freedom, and they behave like responsible people.

American life is full of hypocrisy, a strange mixture of puritanism and excess. If a couple kiss each other on the street in an American city, they are stared at. And in some places they are even asked to stop. In Paris, however, the sight of youth enjoying one of its loveliest experiences is seen with affection. Because of these hypocritical restrictions, the average American girl wants to escape from confinement as soon as she can, and the best way to do that is to acquire a husband. A husband is like a badge she can wear on her chest which says, "See, I have made the club; now I am able to do anything I want." This desire to rush into marriage is why there are so many divorces. American girls marry much too young.

I don't believe a girl should marry until she finds the right person, and knows it deeply. I don't care if she doesņ't marry until she is thirty-five.

Myself, I was born in Poland, the youngest of seven children. I had three sisters and three brothers. There were nine years between myself and the rest. Perhaps I was unwanted, I don't know. My older sisters were of a marriageable age. I wås really the baby of the family. When I was very young—ten—I was sent by my parents to Berlin to study music with an important teacher. I had great difficulties. My music teacher was anti-Polish and anti-Semitic, and I had to fight remarks from him on these subjects. It made things hard on a boy. I had no one to talk with, for the most part, except a wonderful teacher I found when I was eleven or twelve. He gave me great authors like Tolstoy and Gogol to read and he sent me to the theater to see Ibsen and Hauptmann. He opened my mind to many things, to the whole world. By the time I was thirteen, I was independent and completely self-reliant. When my mother wanted me to return to live with my family, I said no. I felt I had to be on my own, and from then on I was.

I had terrible times and wonderful times. When I was seventeen, I fought a duel. I arrived in Paris only by chance and later I came to New York for the first time only because I happened to play the piano at the home of Paderewski; a Boston music critic heard me and made a big halloo in the paper when he returned home. Otherwise, things could easily have gone the other way. I was very depressed at times; once I was on the verge of suicide. Altogether, I had the kind of life that sounds as if it should have been lived in the nineteenth century.

I don't know why I was fortunate enough to survive and develop as I did; I could so easily have gone wrong when I was young. When I had my children, I resolved there was one thing I would do for them. Some fathers say, "I worked for every penny I made. I started at the bottom; you will do the same." But I feel differently. I want to share with my children, while I am alive, the happiness I have found in life, so that in later years they may remember with a warm glow the gaiety, the sunshine and the security they had at home and find strength in those memories at times when they might be sailing in rough seas.

JOAN CRAWFORD

It's Not All Glitter

Joan Crawford has never really given up Hollywood (her last picture was the thriller I Saw What You Did), *although in recent years she has devoted most of her energies to public relations work for Pepsi-Cola, of which company she is a member of the board. Her fabled career as a movie star began when she headed for Hollywood at seventeen, in 1925, determined to be the best dancer in the world. With Jane Kesner Ardmore, she has told her life story in the book* A Portrait of Joan.

One of my teen-age daughters once said to her governess: "I want to be an actress like Mother. I want to have beautiful furs and jewels and dresses. I want everything that goes with being a star."

A few weeks later she had her chance—an opportunity to appear on the Jack Paar TV show. Rehearsal hours were long and strenuous, and after the second day at the studio she came home totally exhausted. "I've changed my mind," she announced. "From now on, I'm just going to borrow everything of Mother's."

My daughter was lucky. She learned quite early in life that there is no shortcut to stardom. Yet I get letters by the thousands from teen-agers who dream of becoming movie stars. Too many of them want only the glitter—

and none of the grind. I think this attitude explains why so many of today's heart-throbs become tomorrow's has-beens. They haven't put in the necessary planning or study or work. And being a celebrity is very hard work. You simply can't be a successful actress—or a successful anything—unless you have a profound desire. I don't mean a desire for the reward, but a desire for the work itself.

Dedication has to come first, but there are three other "musts" for every career girl: good appearance, good speech and good manners. If you don't form these habits when you're in your teens, you never will. Yet they can all be acquired if you set about it in a planned, organized manner.

Let's start with appearance.

Most women look as if they dressed in the dark and made up in a closet. They needn't, for the essence of chic is simplicity. Chic begins with cleanliness—that wonderful sense of being freshly bathed and powdered and perfumed.

The ideal, of course, is to look as if you'd spent your whole day resting and bathing. With organization, you can achieve this look in forty-five minutes.

I often have to change my clothes up to ten times a day, so naturally my wardrobe is large. But it's thoroughly organized. There's not a stitch in it that doesn't belong to an ensemble. In fact, I won't even buy a pair of shoes unless I plan them as part of a complete costume. I build each ensemble about a single item, which is usually the dress. Everything else (hat, bag, shoes, gloves) is subordinate—and coordinate.

Once I've found the look that's right for me, I rarely change it. I have marvelous styles by Irene and Adrian and Jean Louis that I've kept for years without a single alteration, even though the "fashionable" hemline length was bobbing up and down like a yo-yo. Sure it's fun to mimic fashion, but you must modify and always be certain that what you copy is good for *you.*

The same rules apply to make-up. Find your best feature and accent it, without overdoing. The extremes of fashion—big bouffant hairdo, Cleopatra eyes—are for models only, and they look horrendous away from camera. I keep my own make-up simple: just a little powder, eyebrow pencil, mascara, and a light lipstick.

However, you can't pull true glamor from a clothes rack or a make-up kit. I see many smart women who seem to be the height of elegance until they open their mouths. Then bang! goes the illusion, and all I want to do is get out of earshot.

Could you be one of them? It's possible, because most women have naturally piercing voices and they never hear themselves as others hear them. I've had many unique advantages in this area. I've listened to myself in films, learned the ABC's of voice production and studied operatic singing for seven years. But even if you don't have these opportunities, you can still help yourself toward better speech. I think it's an excellent idea, for example, to get your friends together and borrow a tape recorder. Then once you've set the gadget going, just relax and chat and forget about it. The playback can be an ear-opening experience.

Even more important than speaking well is listening well. Frankly, I never like business meetings with other women because most of them have a terribly destructive habit of interrupting. At Pepsi-Cola, I'm the only woman on the board of directors—and it's divine. When we're in conference, I sit there and listen and listen and listen. If I have something to contribute, I wait until the man who's talking has completely finished. Then I raise my hand to speak. I never shout or interrupt but I say my piece in a normal conversational tone. For though a career girl must often think like a man, she must *always* act like a lady. And that brings me to what I think is the most important requisite for the girl who wants to catch the brass ring: manners.

By "manners," I don't simply mean etiquette. I mean

being tough on yourself and gentle with others. Being more interested in what the next person is thinking than in what you yourself have to say. This takes a great deal of discipline, but it's the only way to overcome shyness in a strange situation. Time and again, I'm called upon to talk and act with confidence before a roomful of new people. I'm able to do this by forgetting myself and remembering them.

One last word about manners. A woman in business has an enormous advantage: the fact that men are courteous. They will treat you with respect, listen when you talk and give your opinions priority. This is wonderful, of course, but don't abuse their gallantry. And don't ever, ever use your femininity as a weapon. If you think you can be successful by playing the southern belle or the clinging vine or the *femme fatale—forget it!* You'll be found out in no time flat. The only "role" you should ever play is your own—that of an honest human being.

All of us have something we live by, call it a philosophy or a religion. When I find myself becoming very rushed or frustrated or competitive, I like to remember Ralph Waldo Emerson's definition of true success: To laugh often and love much, to win the respect of intelligent persons and the affection of children, to earn the approbation of honest critics and endure the betrayal of false friends, to appreciate beauty and find the best in others . . . that is success.

DR. J. ROSWELL GALLAGHER

How Much Is It Worth To Win?

Dr. J. Roswell Gallagher is a long-time friend of teen-agers. Currently Chief of the Adolescents' Unit at the Children's Hospital Medical Center in Boston, he received his B.A. from Yale and his M.D. from the Yale School of Medicine. He is the author of Understanding Your Son's Adolescence *and a co-author of* Emotional Problems of Adolescents. *He believes that "kindliness antedates psychiatry by hundreds of years."*

How many times have you heard: "If you're going to *amount to anything* you'd better get high marks," or "If we're going to beat *communism* we've got to learn more math and science"? Hundreds of times, I'm sure. And there's enough truth in these statements so that you can't ignore them. But I'm bothered by their constant din, which at times seems to drown out all else, *and* by our tendency to ignore the evil which lies beneath their surface.

I believe you can do more about this worry of mine than I can, so I would like to tell you why I'm bothered.

Don't get me wrong. I'm not against education, nor for communism. Far from it. It's precisely because I am for democracy that our present-day narrow focus on success, winning and high marks bothers me. Those ends too often seem to justify any means; we seem oblivious to all else.

Nor am I against success. We all need successes if we are to gain enough confidence in ourselves so that we can acquire, and then effectively use, knowledge and skills. Continual failure with no praise makes us retreat from the world and breeds resentment; successes and deserved praise bring contentment and self-respect.

What bothers me is our preoccupation with high marks (desirable as they are), with "getting ahead," with beating the communists (little as we approve their doctrines or aims). We relegate all else—the virtues, beauty, art and *all people who are not successful*—to a second place. So I fear that in our present-day pursuit of excellence, in our efforts to be better than anyone else, we are likely to achieve its shell but fail to gain its substance.

If these are your primary concerns—amounting to something and getting high marks—if you put these first and all else subordinate to them, what may this do to your feminine feelings and attitudes and role, to your regard for what is really good and really important, and to those people who cannot achieve your sort of success? Will you—and others—then regard those who fall short of these goals as failures, as people who have little place in the world and little to contribute? I hope not, for many of them have much more to offer—more compassion and tolerance and understanding—than do some honor students, millionaires and physicists. Are those virtues really second in importance to marks in the nineties, mink coats or nuclear reactors? In our quest for excellence do we need to assign those virtues and the fortunate people who possess them, and all learning that is not "practical," a second place? Is thinking about and trying to understand the world and the role you can play in it only wasting time which could be better spent making money or becoming important or powerful? Is time spent learning to enjoy *"Dulce ridentem Lalagen amabo, dulce loquentem"* * really less likely to improve one's life and the world than studying something "useful"?

The answers are *no*. But if we are to avoid assigning a second place to these people, to these virtues, to learning for its own sake and to art, the job is in large part yours.

It is yours because the pressures of the world around us keep schools busy teaching more and more facts to more and more pupils, and because so many adults strive ceaselessly for survival and success and too few have time to think. And it is yours because youth is the time of not accepting, of doubting, of trying to figure out for oneself. You can do much to set the values straight. You can recognize the good in people who, whether their successes be many or few, have qualities that will make a better world. You can take time to think; to say a kind word; to enjoy or to create something of *value*, though perhaps of little *use;* to admire someone for himself, regardless of his accomplishments; to perfect those attributes which are uniquely feminine.

You can help, too, by remembering the real purpose of education. It is not solely to train the mind. It is to help us to know the world and its people so that we can better it and help some of them; and to teach us how —not what—to think. If those are your goals in school —and in life—you won't dismiss anyone, no matter how unsuccessful or underprivileged, as "not amounting to anything," nor will you give unqualified applause to the unkind valedictorian. Neither will you dismiss art or philosophy or Latin as useless ("Where does it get you?"), nor the Peace Corps as a "waste of time" ("You can get ahead faster if you stay in school"), nor will you join it because "How else could I get to travel?" And most important of all, you will not blindly follow men's ways and goals and studies. You will remember to foster and show

* Still shall I love Lalage and her sweet laughter, Lalage and her sweet prattle—Horace

those feminine qualities which the world so badly needs and which no man can give to it as well as you.

This is the sort of education—of excellence—I hope you will pursue. Don't let anyone tell you that it's only idealism, that while you are thinking or while you are helping someone else, you'll be trampled on. The truly happy—and productive—people in the world care more about the value of what is truly good than about the price it may cost them. Thoreau said it this way: ". . . if one advances confidently in the direction of his dreams, and endeavors to live the life he has imagined, he will meet with a success unexpected in common hours."

MORTON GOULD

What I Think I Remember

Morton Gould, composer, conductor, pianist and arranger, is an extensive contributor to the symphonic band repertory of our schools and colleges. Among his records is Ballet Music of Morton Gould *(which includes* Fall River Legend *and* Interplay, *each a part of the current repertory of the American Ballet Theater and the New York City Ballet, respectively). He is at work with George Balanchine on a new ballet for the New York City Ballet.*

I never quite recovered from adolescence. One rarely does—that is, completely and basically change from what is referred to generally as the "formative years." All years are really formative, as are all conscious living moments, minutes and hours. So in that sense I am a post-post adolescent, a so-called adult. My own adolescence blossomed early. I became seventeen at about the age of thirteen and shortly thereafter a middle-aged teen-ager. The symptoms were typical, and if premature, they were not uncommon.

I had, for example, infinite wisdom and knowledge of things I didn't know, and had conclusive and irrefutable answers to mankind's problems, large and small. Those who agreed were intelligent (like myself), and those who disagreed were stupid. I was on the side of the angels surrounded by Philistines. In the areas that concerned and involved me directly—music, art—my judgment was unencumbered by equivocations. This was great, that was trash, and nothing in between. Compromise was an unspeakable word. There is a whole list of these attitudes, but you know them as well as I do. They are typical of this stage in our living. But certain periods in history, certain times and conditions and happenings can and often do exert an influence. The external pressures of a particular period can shape and mold the internal pressures. My transition through adolescence happened during the famous (or infamous) depression years of the late twenties and thirties. This was a time of grim economic despair and desperation. Able, willing adults were out of work—or selling apples on street corners.

My family's economic status was always tenuous, so in a sense the depression put us in step with everybody else. This was small physical comfort, but at least we shared a common pattern for that time. Strangely enough, being middle-class poor meant that you never admitted the stark fact. So I retain, as do so many others of my generation and upbringing, a vivid recollection of the grim day-by-day struggle and the uncertainty of tomorrow, and the false pride of embarrassment at being poor.

Yet, money or no money, one was growing up and not only dreaming and imagining but talking and discussing and living.

At the age of fifteen I spent a summer at a famous artist's colony in New York. I went because at that time I was actively involved with art as well as music. I was also curious. Then too, I had some older artist friends who were staying there and urging me to "break away." The atmosphere was what is euphemistically called bohemian—or "early beatnik." There were many famous and distinguished artists living in this colony who were up at the crack of dawn and working at their easels. The group in which I found myself was more apt to wake at the crack of noon and resume discussions about art. At a relatively early age I found out the difference between talkers and doers, applicable to any part of living. In order to sustain myself I gave some piano concerts (for which I painted my own posters) and played the piano for dancing classes. There is one thing I have come to realize about that whole mad episode that transcends the many transient incidents of my stay there. One of the reasons I went was to leave my "middle-class," or "bourgeois," family atmosphere. In other words, to escape. Except I am not sure just what I was escaping from. By all the prevalent attitudes my parents should have opposed this venture, or at least have been belligerently unsympathetic. What dramatic reading that would make now—assertively going forth despite parental or social opposition, breaking out from tyranny and repression! Instead, there was no protest or interference—I just went. The irony is that as a parent I doubt that I would do the same. I fancy myself more sophisticated, liberal and understanding than my parents—yet I am not sure that I would be so tolerantly permissive under like circumstances. Pat attitudes and categorical assumptions about people—even parents—are at best presumptuous and at worst untrue.

To get on, I returned home and shortly thereafter left high school—one term short of graduating. I was generally a poor student, but I was already starting to function as a professional musician—sporadic concerts and composing. Perhaps my early adolescence contributed to my unrest but I couldn't wait to get out. Not the least, also, was the economic pressure around me. There wasn't time or leisure to be a student. I was the oldest and therefore first up at bat. This was not an unusual situation of the time; graduating from high school and going to college were not taken for granted. Shortly after leaving high school, I was working in various musical capacities supporting myself and my family. What normally would be a time of dreams and illusions was for me the beginning of reality, the responsibility of surviving.

In memory that whole period is a jumble of events with no remembered specifics or chronology other than swiftly moving experiences in the grown-up professional world. Strangely, one remembers the humorous rather than the distressing. I recall a brief out-of-town engagement as accompanist to a famous "name" act of that time. The leading star allowed me to travel to the city where we were appearing—a three-hour trip—in his chauffeured limousine. He himself came by train. I felt very important traveling in this style to which I was not accustomed. This was during Prohibition, and I found out later that he had had a run-in with some powerful gangster elements and for a while they were literally gunning for him—and watching for his car. In short, I was not only accompanist, but his decoy as well. As it happened, they never spotted his car—otherwise I might not be writing this.

Along with these near-misadventures—and typical of the ambivalence of living—were other happenings. I fell in love—about the age of sixteen. While it lasted it was a cataclysmic seizure. In the light of what I know today, love is many-rooted and rides many waves and is universal. But at the time, I was the sole discoverer of this phenomenon. It was what the romantic literature alludes to as a *Sturm und Drang*—storm and stress—romance. There were melodramatic partings, letters, phone calls, reconciliations, accusations, threats of self-destruction—all, incidentally, justified on both sides.

And now, the practical intrudes again. Oh, the love interest continues—but we have arrived at my eighteenth birthday and a "permanent" job: staff musician at the then new Radio City Music Hall in New York City. This was a seven-day-week position—four to six shows a day, starting mornings and continuing to late evening. I was lucky, at the time, to get this relative security, but it was the end of my adolescence. In a sense I'm ahead of the game—if life is a race. And in a way it is, at least against time—that relentless and unending movement that magnetizes all of us at all ages and through every age of man. Our calendars, clocks, anniversaries and memorials are proof of this recognition. Yet one doesn't come too far away from the adolescent. Maturing is not really changing, but rather tempering, controlling, diverting, modifying and at times perhaps intensifying.

Not too long ago, I received a bundle of letters written by me to a close friend during the adolescent years I have just described. I was struck by the fact that barring some melodramatic passages here and there they could have been written by me today. I was fundamentally and chemically the same person. I even predicted, fairly accurately, the results of certain attitudes I had and directions I was going. It is amazing how we can listen and not truly hear ourselves and shape our lives accordingly. I regret not finishing high school and attending college. I consider myself reasonably intelligent—but I lack intellectual discipline (though I know academically disciplined people who are not intelligent). I regret the expediencies, the compromises. Yet could one really undo one tile without changing the whole mosaic? And then we would have cause to regret all over again, but for different reasons. So let's just leave it as "I regret." The moment one utters these words, it is too late anyway.

Now to the satisfactions. There is, of course, my music —which is a natural, living part of me. All of me comes together when I compose and this in itself is a fulfilling experience. But in terms of personal and human satisfaction there is my family—my wife and children. The thought and sight of them warms my heart, and this is as real and stimulating and rewarding an experience as one can have—if fortunate enough. I know this family story doesn't fire a dramatic book or play—but it ignites one's life and glows with time's passing. For this I am deeply grateful.

If I could live my life over again, in all probability I would do the same things in one way or another, mistakes and all. Even were time run backward, I don't think we could retrieve; it is the nature of our own limitations at different ages and stages. The one possible thought I offer is that the act of conscious living requires discipline, not for its own sake, but in terms of control, selection and discrimination. This is how one sets a course and a direction, both in personal living and professional achievement. This is how we develop our muscles to help move us forward to our respective horizons.

PHILIP ROTH

They Won't Make You Normal

Philip Roth, who won the National Book Award in 1960 for his first collection of short stories, Goodbye, Columbus, *was born in Newark, New Jersey, in 1933. His first novel,* Letting Go, *was published in 1962. After a year as Writer-in-Residence at Princeton University, he is now at work on a novel and two plays.*

A fourteen-year-old boy I know once asked me, "Why bother reading novels?" He had been having to spend much of his summer plowing through some long books assigned to him by his school, and I suppose he was crabbing as much as inquiring. Nevertheless, his question is finally an intelligent one, as are many crabby questions that begin, "Why bother—?" Young people who want to take themselves seriously have a right to ask "Why?" and "What for?" about any human activity, and particularly, I would think, about those activities that adults always suggest are "good for you."

Novel reading isn't "good for you" anyway. Brushing your teeth is good for you; eating raw vegetables is good for you; keeping your feet dry is good for you, et cetera, et cetera. What is normally considered good for teen-agers is what keeps your temperature normal, your behavior normal and, above all, your attitudes normal, safe and unexplosive. Beware of the man (or woman) who tells you, "Do it because it is good for you"; often the only person it is good for is him (or her).

Why I heartily recommend to you the reading of novels (and the writing of them, if you are feeling game) is that, according to the standards of "normalcy," it is undoubtedly bad for you. Novels do not pussyfoot around. They can leave you sulky, angry, fearful and desperate. They can leave you dissatisfied with the life you are living. Sometimes, upon finishing a book, you can't help but dislike yourself—for being smug or narrow or callous or unambitious, for sharing in any of the hundreds of ways in which we are all of us without feeling or without understanding. Novels can make you skeptical and doubting—of your friends, of your family, of your religion, of your country; they can reveal to you that the kind of person you happen to be or think you want to be isn't really worth being. If you want to do what is good for you, please don't read novels. Or if you simply have to, read popular novels of that sort that suggest that if you are a good person you will be happy and loved, and if you are a bad person you will go to an early grave.

Now it isn't my intention to suggest that novels have "messages" and that you should read only the ones with whose "messages" I concur. Young people (and old people) who ask me if I write because I have a message tempt me to reply: "No, that is why I send telegrams." A writer of fiction is not a minister giving a sermon or a parent giving advice. Fiction isn't simply another way of telling people how to behave—at least, not fiction written by mature people for other mature people to read. I am afraid that the reader has missed the thrill of novel reading if he comes away from a book saying, "The writer is trying to tell us that we should all do this, or we shouldn't do that." The writer is not trying to tell us what we should and should not do; hopefully, he is trying to reveal what it is we *do* do, and do not do.

That is why I indicated earlier that the reading of

a novel may be an upsetting experience. For as you probably know, the reasons we offer ourselves to explain our daily actions to ourselves may not always be the reasons that are driving us to act. Sometimes we deliberately deceive ourselves; sometimes we deliberately deceive others; somtimes we are blind to the cause and the consequence of what we are doing. Life is not simply choosing to do what is good and choosing not to do what is bad, for there are times in the life of a boy or a girl, or a man or a woman, when despite all the best intentions, he cannot tell which is which. To have to live is to have to take a chance. Sorry, but that is the condition that we are saddled with. And since it is, we might as well try to understand it—and that is why some people write novels, and why other people read them.

Of course, this is also why people read and write books on philosophy, religion, art, history, psychology and physics, books that are not novels, but which inform us deeply about the character of man and the nature of our world. I wouldn't want to conclude with any of you imagining that the novelist's ultimate goal is to transmit information. That is what an encyclopedia or a newspaper does. It is not the facts of life alone that concern the novelist, it is the *feel* of life. Whatever his style, his setting or his subject, his task as a writer is to pursue the mysteries of life to their very source. At least, to try to. It does not matter, either, if the reader cannot, as the expression goes, "sympathize with the characters" or "identify" with them. For it is not the reader's job to put limitations upon the writer's imagination, but the writer's job to liberate the imagination of the reader. If I am permitted to write only about what the reader can bring himself to sympathize with, then how can I ever get the reader to see that there is perhaps more to life than what *his* eyes reveal to him? What is crucial to the novelist is not the reader's sympathy, but his *belief*. Even when you read of characters who are in no way like what you consider yourself to be, and of events unlike any you may yet have lived through, you should be able to say, "Ah yes, that is true, that is the way that it is."

You should be able to say this, to be sure, only if the novelist has done his job. And now, I should like to have the pleasure of presenting to you a list of ten novels that are decidedly not good for you—they won't make you "normal"—and that is why I want to recommend them. If you want to read books showing that life is all honey and roses, and tra-la-la, it's eternally spring, then you might just as well read no further.

Winesburg, Ohio,
by Sherwood Anderson

Mrs. Bridge,
by Evan Connell

The Great Gatsby,
by F. Scott Fitzgerald

Madame Bovary,
by Gustave Flaubert

The Lord of the Flies,
by William Golding

The Assistant,
by Bernard Malamud

The Lonely Passion of Judith Hearne,
by Brian Moore

Lie Down in Darkness,
by William Styron

Anna Karenina,
by Leo Tolstoy

Look Homeward, Angel,
by Thomas Wolfe

I do not know if these are "books for teen-agers," because that is not how I think of books. I do not know if they are books for young men or books for young women, for I don't think that, in reading, that distinction is an important one, once you are on your way to maturity. What I do know is that these are novels which deal with human beings seeking to discover (because life forces you to discover) what it is to *be* a human being. Some of the characters in these books find out, if not what it is to be human, at least what it is *not* to be; their stories are not pleasant or "light," nor do they have happy endings. I do not know if every single teen-ager is going to understand every single page of every one of these books; I seriously doubt it. If you want to understand every page of a book, your best bet is to go back and read over the books you read two years ago. If you want to move ahead now, I hope you'll try one or two of the books I've suggested. Actually, what I hope is that you'll try all ten.

PETE SEEGER

Dear Fellow Humans:

Pete Seeger, son of a musicologist father and a violinist mother, has been strumming his guitar and banjo and singing his songs, cheering people up for more than two decades. He has edited a songbook, American Favorite Ballads as Sung by Pete Seeger; *his recent Columbia albums are* We Shall Overcome *and* God Bless the Grass.

I usually mistrust older people's giving advice to younger, because while often their advice is very good (the values of foresight, temperance, persistence, etc.), they forget that younger people usually know one of the most important things of all: the value of enthusiasm and enjoyment of life.

Twenty-five years ago Franklin Roosevelt spoke to my generation. "Youth: Hold fast to your dreams," he said. In other words don't give up your ideals of peace, freedom, justice, truth—the way so many adults do. When you come down to it, more people die from discouragement than from any disease. And why do people get discouraged? Because they feel that life's a joyless struggle; because they feel they're on a dead-end street.

So here are a few of my own recipes for avoiding this kind of discouragement. They may or may not apply to you. Only you can decide.

1. It's better to take a job you want at less pay than a job you don't want for more pay. But you can learn from any job.

2. It's okay to suffer intense temporary discomforts in order to reach a longer-range goal. But make sure it is only temporary.

3. Debts can be chains, best used when they can haul you to new heights, rather than entangle your legs. It's the same with possessions: "Man doesn't possess possessions; they possess us."

4. Travel while you are young and still are free of responsibilities. See what a big, broad, beautiful land we have here, then maybe a foreign land or two. See that there are honest, hard-working people in every corner of the globe, all quite certain that their own way of living, their local geography, their music, etc., is the most beautiful.

5. Keep your health. It's easy while you are young. But our fine, tempting, modern civilization can erode it easily too. Many a man or woman has finally worked himself into a position in which he could do something, and then found he no longer had the health to do it or enjoy it.

5½. In view of the fact that good health and energy don't last forever, it's worth doing some things earlier than later. When my wife and I were about thirty and very broke, we built our own house, inch by inch, on a mountainside. Glad we did: doubt we'd have energy enough to do it now. And I've known too many people who put off such projects "until we have the money" or "until we have the time"—and if they eventually did get the money or the time, they no longer had the energy.

6. A happy sex life may take years to achieve, but it's worth it in the long run. Worth the time, the thought— or rather, the thoughtfulness—and, often, the waiting.

7. A few short ones: Prestige is much overrated. The celebrity business is for the birds. Respectability is nice, but consider: whom do you most want to respect you? Money is like air or water. You need a certain amount

to live. Beyond that, who wants to be a dog in the manger?

And now I'll stop before I rattle on any longer, like any old graybeard. All the foregoing applies to the one central thing I mentioned at the beginning: how to keep discouragement from withering the priceless enthusiasm which most young people have.

So far I've quoted F.D.R. and Ralph Waldo Emerson. Here are a few more favorite quotes. (Note: When you steal from one person, it's plagiarism. When you steal from ten, it's scholarship. When you steal from a hundred, it's original research.)

First, a story about the late comedian Fred Allen. He once saw a small boy toddle in front of a truck and snatched him to safety just in time. On the sidewalk again, he said, "S'matter, kid—don't you want to grow up and have troubles?"

Next, a fragment from the German poet Bertolt Brecht:

> . . . For we know only too well:
> Even the hatred of squalor
> Makes the brow grow stern;
> Even anger against injustice
> Makes the voice grow harsh. Alas, we
> Who wished to lay the foundations of · kindness
> Could not ourselves be kind.*

Here's a famous line credited to Gandhi: "To the millions who have to go without two meals a day, the only form in which God dare appear is food." A line from a Harvard graduate back from Africa: "Nigerians are a proud people who don't want tourists, don't want heroes, don't want saviors. They just want schoolteachers."

Now, a paragraph from Woody Guthrie, the dustbowl balladeer, who taught me much not only about music but about my country and life in general:

"The worst thing that can happen to you is to cut yourself loose from people. And the best thing is to sort of

---

* From *Selected Poems of Bertolt Brecht,* translated by H. R. Hays, copyright 1947 by Bertolt Brecht and H. R. Hays. Reprinted by permission of Harcourt, Brace & World, Inc.

vaccinate yourself right into the bloodstreams of the people . . . to feel that you know the best and the worst of folks that you see everywhere, and never to feel weak, or lost, or even lonesome anywhere . . . There is just one thing that can cut you to drifting from the people, and that's any brand or style of greed . . . There is just one way to save yourself, and that's to get together and work and fight for everybody." *

Lastly, I quote the words of a song I put together a few years ago, using words from the Book of Ecclesiastes.

> To everything (turn, turn, turn)
> There is a season (turn, turn, turn)
> And a time for every purpose
> Under heaven.
>
> A time to be born, a time to die,
> A time to plant, a time to reap,
> A time to kill, a time to heal,
> A time to laugh, a time to weep.
>
> A time to dance, a time to mourn,
> A time to build up, a time to break down,
> A time to cast away stones,
> A time to gather stones together.
>
> A time of love, a time of hate,
> A time of war, a time of peace,
> A time you may embrace,
> A time to refrain from embracing.
>
> A time to gain, a time to lose,
> A time to rend, a time to sew,
> A time to love, a time to hate,
> A time for peace—I swear, it's not too late!
>
> To everything (turn, turn, turn)
> There is a season (turn, turn, turn)
> And a time for every purpose
> Under heaven.†

* Used by permission of the Guthrie Children's Trust Fund.
† *To Everything There Is a Season (Turn! Turn! Turn!)* Words from the Book of Ecclesiastes. Adaptation and music by Pete Seeger. Copyright 1962, Melody Trails, Inc., New York, N.Y. Used by permission.

Well, here's hoping all the foregoing will help you avoid a few dead-end streets (we all hit some), and here's hoping enough of your dreams come true to keep you optimistic about the rest. We've got a big world to learn how to tie together. We've all got a lot to learn. And don't let your studies interfere with your education.

Sincerely,

Pete Seeger

JOAN SUTHERLAND

Singing in a Tree

Joan Sutherland began studying voice in her native Australia and continued in England, where she joined the Covent Garden Opera Company. She won stardom with her superb singing of Lucia di Lammermoor, *and she has since appeared at many of the world's opera houses. Among her London opera recordings are* The Age of Bel Canto, *Bellini's* I Puritani *and* La Sonnambula, *Verdi's* La Traviata, *Handel's* Alcina *and Donizetti's* Lucia di Lammermoor.

If there is one thing I would really like to do, it's to write a nice long article about some subject that has nothing whatsoever to do with music—just for a change—but after considering innumerable subjects I am forced to the conclusion that I am lacking in qualifications. So I shall simply "reflect."

When I was young I used to sit myself in a tree in our garden and sing to the birds. They were a critical audience and if they did not approve left me singing to myself. So then I'd sing to the flowers—at least they couldn't walk out. I think singing in trees must be a family characteristic, as my mother did the same thing when she was young. Once she left her stage rather precipitately and was rescued by her father after a neighbor had reported that "your little girl is hanging head down out of a tree."

The incident certainly didn't affect her—she had a beautiful voice even when she was over seventy.

All my family sang—some in key, others more original in their vocal renditions. My Uncle Tom was one member who "performed." His repertoire was extensive and divided; he sang in the church choir on Sundays and anywhere else on weekdays. I believe his dramatic intensity was superb when he delivered "My Old Woman's an Awful Boozer," a scene obviously drawn from the weekday repertoire.

Mother attended to all my early vocal training. She thought I had the makings of a dramatic soprano, as did my first "official" teachers in both Australia and England. Richard Bonynge, my husband, whom I met in Australia when I was in my teens, thought differently. I would sing around the house and slip up into the higher notes without realizing what I was doing. He decided if I could do it around the house, I could do it on the stage—and that started a battle of no mean dimensions. He won.

We've traveled to places in many parts of the world since those days—really not so very long ago; we've had many "ups" and quite a few "downs," but what I liked most was the sharing of our various experiences.

I've sung Lucia, the poor demented bride of Lammermoor, in at least a dozen different opera houses all over the world—each time the scenery and costumes (except my own) changed with the country and the people's own ideas of Scotland. In Barcelona the soldier's sporrans were worn as little white aprons around their waists, but even so, this was a definite improvement on a much earlier production when, had the soldiers been required to sit, the sporrans wouldn't have been seen at all. Also one soldier, feeling the cold a little, wore his long underwear beneath the kilt. Although the exterior of the castle changed, the ballroom changed, and my brother Henry was variously Australian, Welsh, American, Italian, Spanish and French, I enjoyed working with them all.

People often say to me, "You are lucky, seeing all those places." Only I see very little of "all those places." The inside of certain hotel rooms and the opera houses I could probably describe in minute detail, but there are many wonderful things to be seen that, as yet, I've not had time to visit. In Milan, for instance, I've stayed on and off over a long period, and each visit I think that this time I'll take myself off to see Leonardo da Vinci's famous painting of the Last Supper in the church of Santa Maria delle Grazie. I think I have just said it for the seventh time. On the other hand I had a glorious tourist's week in Palermo when the stagehands at the theater went on strike.

Quite often I am asked to write my most thrilling, humorous, embarrassing and so on experiences. These questions aren't always easy to answer. My most embarrassing experiences are quite unprintable and bad enough when I think of them, without seeing them down in black and white. Really humorous experiences are somewhat rare, as they tend to become mixed with the embarrassing. Fortunately I've never found a sense of humor missing in an opera company, and mostly we can all enjoy an incident, whether personally involved or not. Thrilling experiences now are so numerous I find great difficulty in choosing one above the rest. However, one that will always live with me was the acceptance in Venice of Handel's opera *Alcina*. Handel is not a general favorite of the Italian people, a situation which made their acclaim of this long-forgotten opera such a heart-warming event.

Some audiences are warmer than others. I have certainly found no lack of warmth or of generosity in America's theaters and concert halls. One is always assured of a fair and reasonable criticism, which is really all an artist asks.

My reflections have been of events that have passed. Of the future? I hope I may sing for many years—improve my technique, revive forgotten operas, sing many roles which, as yet, I have only thought of doing, and between times listen to other vocalists and instrumentalists and augment our collection of music and old books. And I hope, even if I live to be seventy, that I shall never lose the urge to study, for the world of entertainment is demanding, and it demands always the best one is capable of giving.

ROY WILKINS

The Spirit of '76 in the 1960's

Roy Wilkins is executive director of the National Association for the Advancement of Colored People, a national organization with an interracial membership whose goal is the end of racial discrimination and segregation.

Born in St. Louis, Missouri, in 1901, Mr. Wilkins spent his childhood in the Twin City of St. Paul, Minnesota. He joined the staff of the NAACP in 1931 as assistant executive secretary and served simultaneously as editor of The Crisis, its monthly magazine, until he assumed his present leadership.

In my home state of Minnesota, far from the deep South, I remember well that I was stirred in my teen years by the lynching of a circus roustabout in a town uncomfortably close to the Twin Cities. I had read of such acts elsewhere, but here it was on my doorstep.

Many young Americans today are taking their Americanism seriously because racism laps at the doorstep of everything they and their country hold dear. Others may smirk or scoff at the line in our immortal Declaration of Independence, but not this new breed. To them the great ideas of freedom are not just words:

". . . all men are created equal . . . are endowed by their Creator with certain unalienable Rights . . . among these are Life, Liberty and the pursuit of Happiness. That to secure these rights, Governments are instituted among Men, deriving their just powers from the consent of the governed."

Millions of Americans learned those words and believed them. The trouble was that few persons considered that the sentiment applied to Negro Americans who for three generations had been outside the guarantees of the Constitution in the South and, in varying degrees, in the North also.

American teen-agers and young adults have sparked the modern drive for human rights. The white young people responded to the Macedonian cry of the Negro young people because that call for aid was at once a call to Americanism and a challenge to the heart.

This young army is marked by study and questioning, by dedicated conviction and by action. Teen-agers saw a wrong and worked at righting it by taking part in a project in their school, neighborhood or city. They raised and sent funds to the front-line areas.

Young white people joined Negro youth in questioning what theretofore had been routine procedure. When the famed sit-ins began in the late fifties and swept the nation in the early sixties, white teen-agers were ready for more than debate. To the consternation and dismay of southern whites and to the apprehension and pride of northerners, they joined in the demonstrations.

They were arrested and jailed. They were insulted and physically attacked. Two of them, Andrew Goodman and Michael Schwerner, joined their Negro co-worker, James Chaney, in martyrdom when the three were killed in cold blood in Mississippi in 1964. White young people were in Selma and Montgomery, Alabama, in 1965. They discovered inequalities they never knew existed. They were left aghast and angry at calculated cruelty, at implacable race hatred. They witnessed firsthand a political, economic and social system that is a travesty on the freedoms set forth in our Constitution. They came to know and to marvel at the ingenuity and quiet courage of the exploited Negro and to understand the dilemma of those white southerners who were heartsickened, but remained silent and immobile.

Yes, the American white teen-agers have put their stamp upon the Changing Sixties. Not all of them understand the whole problem, but they do know that the old excuses and the old ways are unacceptable.

From tree-shaded campuses over the land, from the east and west coasts, from the south and the north, the youth of our nation is serving notice that it intends to redeem the good name of the country it loves.

It is making the land over, not into a new image, but into the old image that prompted 1776, the Civil War and Amendments Thirteen, Fourteen and Fifteen and two bloody wars to make the world safe for democracy and to destroy Hitlerism.

The emerging image is shining and hopeful, with layers of hypocrisy and suspicion and myth removed from the minds and hearts of white and black Americans.

The teen-agers are sure they want an America that is honest and courageous in facing up to the racial problem. In this they are following not only their priests, ministers and rabbis, their teachers and other counselors, but their President, Lyndon B. Johnson, who declared in a moving civil rights speech in 1965:

"So we want to open the gates to opportunity. But we are also going to give all our people—black and white— the help they need . . . It never ever occurred to me in my fondest dreams (in 1928) that I might have a chance to help . . . But now I do have that chance and I will let you in on a secret—I mean to use it. And I hope you will use it with me."

And as a purely personal and selfish but satisfying

footnote, let me add that these brave young people are gladdening a once teen-age heart that in 1919 looked vainly but worked doggedly for the awakening and the outrage and the action that took so long to get here and is, therefore, blessedly welcome.

LARRY RIVERS

Dear Teen-age Audience:

Larry Rivers, a brilliant painter whose canvases and sculptures are impregnated with his lively ideas, was born in New York City. Before committing himself to his present career, he made the scene playing the jazz saxophone; he had no knowledge of art until a fellow jazzman showed him a painting of a bass fiddle by Georges Braque. Two years later he began studying with Hans Hoffmann, and in 1949 he had a one-man show, the first of many both here and abroad. He is represented in the collections of New York's Museum of Modern Art, the Whitney Museum of American Art, the Kansas City Museum and other leading museums.

In order to impress you by praise or criticism or with any of the clichés available to me I have to imagine an audience. So what is a teen-ager? A shy faceful of red welts, a brown, black or blond version of Sue Lyons' Lolitasville, an earnest seeker of personal truth in the shape of either the "beautiful" or "terribly distorted." Is it my son? Sons, I mean, one who begged to quit school and lowers his voice when he smells judgment, whose self-pity bears a pretty reasonable relationship to his tragedy called "My Life." If you tell me your age is a tough one, I'll immediately construct something to inspire big booming doubts: for you are removed (except perhaps by over-hearing) from the tedious jungle of money, rent, food and blah blah. The mirror sends back: no wrinkles, a sturdy hair and jaw line embellished in beautiful lazy summers, and death is far, far away—almost as if it didn't really exist. But if you hand me the PTA–*Ladies' Home Journal* line of sweet sweaters, puffball cuddle and "teen talk" by the giggleful I'll arrange another picture for you which only the wooden and the blind could take for bliss. It can be quite an unfunny picture of how lost you are and how sandy everything really feels. I can even talk you into being without legs. But don't fret. I'm only here to impress you! You know, the forty-year-old experienced pipeful-of-affection-for-the-young with lots of advice about how to live a full, and if possible rich, "arty" life (since I'm an artist) and that there are eternal values and they are the property of all. *"Seek and ye shall find."* I'm not Norman Vincent Peale. No. I'm Larry Vincent Peale. Truth in a modern form all wrapped up for you in the innocence of tough talk.

1. If you have no answer for your mother's sacrifices—she was a genius and she made them (the sacrifices) seem real—tell her about *her* mother. If she's one of those that has had it good and thick on both ends—that is, she was a grateful daughter *and* a sacrificing mother—just give her up as hopeless.

2. For girls. Your father might be in love with you but remember that's because it is impossible.

3. For boys. I carried bags of vegetables and fruit for three cents a bag and gave my mother the money at the end of the week for her tap on the head. We have no way of knowing if we are not going from one horrible head tapping to another. It might be better than robbing your mother's purse, but I did that too.

I think I'm still carrying those bags. Oh, it looks like something else; the price I get per bag is higher and the bags have become paintings and sculpture and, of course, all sorts of hands reach out and tap, but you work and 86 then you wait for a soothing "Good boy," "Very good," "Yes." I hope you're not getting the idea that I think as a kid I was a "good" boy and now that I'm forty I'm being bitter about it. Not at all. After a certain age, say twenty-three or the point at which you no longer can use your parents, everything to do with them is memory. You look at this accident and in relation to your sweet-sour soul you make up a giant clam chowder. At my age on evenings that wind their way slowly up the trail of family memories you warm up this chowder just enough to keep things bouncing. And if you are young and you've left that small town because to go down in history in Speonk or Dutchmaster, Tennessee, as a ballet dancer seems like a little "too much," and the one or two members of the opposite sex that you've flung yourself at in the big city say *"You?"* . . . and after a few other difficulties in trying to live a pleasurable and glamorous life hurry you off to the analyst's couch, you can drag out endless portions for the one or two years needed to iron out the difficulties. Maybe for a novel you might write. Otherwise there is hardly anything to be done with this soup. Surely you can't make things "right" with your parents.

But you are there and I, alas, am over here, and that is the difficulty. At fifteen you push your hair forward. At sixteen to the side and up. Lots of goo and lots of cute sassy speeches at the nonbelievers and no memory about having been fifteen years old. At seventeen your hair could be straight back and flat and the same lips and eyes form for its defense and propagation. And you are right and you are wrong. You are right because it is your face and hair and lips, etc., and with it you must devise some quality of being, but you are wrong because in your case the results can be *ugh oof bong horrible* and you can't really suffer and also because the reasons for your choice are obvious and singularly unoriginal. A mannequin (though willing) of collective pressure.

However, don't let this intimidate you. In the late 1930's I wore pants so wide at the knees that two of my friends could have stayed there with me and, shoeless, I could hardly squeeze through at the bottom. Long jacket, long collar, long hair and later on bebop cap—in fact the complete "groover." I imagined that the more I resembled the Negro jazz musicians—what they wore and the way they spoke and what they indulged in—the better my saxophone playing would become. "My hero!" But I'm being rather kind to myself here. Back a little, *you* give in to the collective image, just wanting to "look like" something (calms you down about differences) and little else. *I* present *myself* as wanting to look like something only in order to *become* something else. Which is obviously a more worthwhile involvement and which is obviously full of the muck and pomposity you are handed out everywhere you go, and free! Mind me now! The message is a-comin'.

The better you are able to discern what is going on in connection with your parents and some silly teachers, in magazine articles about success, in politics, etc., and finally in yourself, the angrier you will become. You may think life is all about getting calm and happy but not yet. Not for you. And there's nothing wrong with that anger and you needn't even be neat about where you put it. If you have "greatness" in mind you will worry, and you might as well begin now, for just "plain old you" ain't enough. Write me.

Affectionately,
Larry Rivers

MAX LERNER

On Resuming the Dialogue

PHILIPPE HALSMAN

Max Lerner is professor of American Civilization and World Politics at Brandeis University and writer of a syndicated newspaper column which appears widely in the United States and many other countries. A graduate of Yale, he has taught at Sarah Lawrence, Williams and Harvard. His book America as a Civilization *is a basic text in many colleges. He has also written of* The Age of Overkill.

A long time in the future a historian, looking back at our time, may call it the time when the dialogue stopped. I mean, of course, the dialogue between the generations, the channels through which the younger people and the older people keep their universes in touch with each other. There has always been a generational struggle of some kind. Our parents broke away from our grandparents, who in turn had broken away from their elders. There has always been grief on each side as a consequence, and a conflict that has grated on the nerves of each.

Actually there is nothing wrong with conflict. Quarrels don't trouble me much, whether between husband and wife or between parents and children or between friends; they are a sign that the relationship is still alive. What is much worse is complete silence and estrangement—the breakdown of the dialogue, when nothing is said because there is nothing much to be said, or because we have forgotten how to say it, or because our universes have moved so far apart that the gap between them has become unbridgeable. The great trouble in our time is the ending of the dialogue between the generations.

How can we manage to resume it? The first step is to be aware of the need. We have heard much about the "dropouts" from high school or college, who leave school too early to plunge into a world outside. In another sense a large segment of the younger generation has dropped out of the society of the adults and out of its assumptions and values—perhaps because they feel in their own hearts that the adults have dropped out of *their* world and values. Every so often I meet people who are absorbed in the question of interplanetary communication. "Isn't there some message that they are trying to send to us from outer space?" they ask me. My answer is that there is a message which our own teens are trying to send to us, not from outer space but from within our own homes, our own high schools and colleges, our own cities. I try to tell them that nobody seems to be listening.

That is the first key to resuming the dialogue: to listen. It sounds easy, but it isn't. It is almost a lost art because you can't listen if you are angry or scared or anxious or sullen or preoccupied with your own problems. I have seen few parents who listen to their children; mostly they scold or nag or harry them with questions. And teens don't listen to adults because they doubt that the adults have anything to say that is worth listening to. Our trouble is that we make the TV set the center of the home instead of the kitchen refrigerator. For the TV set drowns out communication, but the refrigerator is what the youngsters can raid when they get home, usually pretty late, and sitting around the kitchen table they can tell what happened and swap experiences, and both sides can listen.

Listening involves openness—to other persons, to experience, to ideas. There are few people who lay themselves open to others in this sense. A good teacher does, because for him every student is a bundle of potentials that he wants to explore. You can spot an adult with whom the dialogue is possible: He will have curiosity about books, plays, music, far places, the past and future and not just the present; he won't play judge or censor, constantly moralizing at you, constantly passing judgment on you; but neither will he curry favor with you or try to become a teen-ager himself. He will be exactly who he is, an adult open to your experience, willing to tell you of the sting of his own experience and his memory of joys and sorrows, of the mistakes he has made as well as the triumphs he has had. And you can open the dialogue with him if you are willing to put your puzzlements and confusions to him, knowing that he is not there to judge you.

The trouble with many parents is that life has shut them up tight, like a clam. I don't mean verbally (some of us talk far too much), but emotionally. The worst parental crime against teen-agers is to give them a loveless home to grow up in—a home in which the children and adults are strangers because the husband and wife themselves are strangers to each other. I have seen parents who ask why their teen-agers don't seem to love them or talk to them, forgetting that they have grown up in a home environment denuded of any affectionate life and any genuine emotional expressiveness. What they forget is that the dialogue is not something you can turn on and off like a water tap. It is something that must grow, something the parents should have started long ago, while the children were young. The longer they wait, the harder it will be to resume.

Many adults feel that some sort of devil has entered into the minds of the younger generation, distorting and corrupting them. They need to get rid of this myth of diabolism. The fact is that something like a youth culture has emerged in American life, with values that are different from adult values although at some points they intersect. To resume the dialogue each generation must try to enter the intellectual and moral universe of the other. This will mean reading some of the same books, listening to some of the same records, going to some of the same plays and movies. The great cultural explosions of our age, including a new spate of paperbacks and LP's, makes this possible for the first time.

I end with the question of distrust and trust. A paralyzing distrust has settled down between the generations. "Don't trust anyone over thirty" was the way one student leader put it, during the Berkeley sitdown. I know many adults who don't trust anyone under twenty. Young people need a sense of fidelity. They have a hunger to trust someone and to be trusted, because unless you trust someone else you can't trust yourself. The generations can't start trusting each other overnight, turning fidelity on like a shower in the morning. We can resume the dialogue only by trusting each other on particular concrete matters, one occasion of trust leading to another, one growing from another, the small doses of trust all mounting to a dialogue in which people are open and listen and are emotionally expressive and enter into each other's world.

JEAN DALRYMPLE

Make Up Your Mind

Jean Dalrymple, player, playwright, publicist and producer, has made a career out of her love for the theater. At seventeen she starred in a comedy sketch on the vaudeville circuits; with the end of big-time vaudeville, she found work on Broadway as an understudy, casting director, play doctor and press agent. Currently she heads the New York City Center Light Opera and Drama companies. Her entertaining autobiography is called September Child.

Seventeen is a darling age. You have left the uncertainties and dependencies of childhood but have not yet taken up the responsibilities of an adult. It is an age to enjoy, to savor and to appreciate, especially if you are a girl, because then you are lovely. Everything about you is fresh and springlike—your body, your mind and your soul. Life has not had time to thicken your waistline, muddle your thoughts or corrode your psyche.

Seventeen is also a time when you can shape your whole life to come. It is the time of decision. This is just as true for boys.

My husband graduated from high school when he was seventeen and he had the good fortune to have his choice of going to Annapolis, West Point or majoring in economics at Harvard University. He chose West Point and never regretted it. Not even, as he put it, when he was shot at from across the street while taking the town of Huertgen, Germany, in World War II, or when his helicopter was attacked when he was commanding general of the famous Thunderbirds in the Korean War.

I made a decision, too, when I was seventeen.

When I was very little—not more than nine or ten, I'd say—I wanted to be a writer. When I proudly announced my ambition, I was deflated at being told that every little girl wants to be a writer. After brooding about this for a time, I decided that all the other little girls might have wanted to write, but I had written and would write. Actually I had already dramatized and had performed in Sunday School two Bible stories, Ruth, and Joseph and His Coat of Many Colors, and had been a regular contributor to children's magazines and newspaper pages. And so I continued my tiny but to me satisfying "career" until, being eager to get out into the world and to "live," as I put it to myself, I went to work in Wall Street when I was barely sixteen. Having nothing more important in my head, I soaked up effortlessly and intuitively the ways and mores of the financial world. I was happy, successful and satisfied, except for one thing—I had no time or urge to write.

Then in that fateful seventeenth year, I was offered an extraordinary and unsought opportunity: to embark on a different career, as an actress, and with a company which was starting out on what unfolded to me as a glamorous and exciting six months' tour of our beautiful continent from coast to coast.

If it is said that all little girls want to be writers, it is also said that all young girls want to be actresses. The latter was not my case. I still wanted to be a writer. Again intuitively, I felt that the stimulus of travel and the company of theater people would start my typewriter to turning out something besides business letters. I was right. First I wrote sketches—one-act plays for vaudeville and then scripts for two-reel "talkies," so popular in those days—and finally a full-length play.

It was this play, produced by John Golden, which put me firmly in the world of the performing arts—a world which I have never left and have never regretted entering. The first step was made, however, when I was seventeen.

For some people coming to a decision at any age is difficult. I have known a few who find it virtually impossible. I know one otherwise brilliant woman who can't even decide what she wants to eat when we have lunch together. After interminable, agonizing moments with the waiter standing on one foot and then the other, she eventually ends up with, "I'll have whatever you have."

This same woman recently brought herself to the point of a nervous collapse when she redecorated her house and her office. White walls or blue-gray? Wall-to-wall carpeting or a new rug? I listened to her on the telephone for hours because I love her, but I could throttle her.

Most indecision is caused by fear, and F.D.R.'s famous words, "The only thing we have to fear is fear itself," hold particularly true here. At seventeen you may not be faced with any life-making or -breaking choices, but it is a good idea to start thinking positively and decisively in small choices so that the habit grows with you as the years pass. You will save countless ergs of mental energy and nervous strain.

For instance, start right in when you are replenishing your wardrobe. At seventeen your mother should no longer be doing this for you. Shopping is exhausting only when you start out with a haphazard notion of what you need and what you like, and for goodness' sake, if you're a girl, make up your mind beforehand to buy only those things which are becoming to you. If green makes you feel and look bilious, don't wear it because all the other girls look dandy in it. Don't wear stretch pants if you haven't the figure for them (although almost all seventeens have!).

There I go making decisions for you! But in this case

it's offered as advice and that is always something to be considered when you are making up your own mind. The ability to weigh advice (and you will get tons and tons of it as you go through life) and not be confused by it is a vital asset and also can be developed.

It is hard even to listen to advice when you are seventeen because when it comes from an older generation, you are quick to conclude that "things were different when they were my age."

Actually the fundamental things haven't changed at all. Older people know all too well how the world is changing and how the changes affect the outward part of your life. They've been all through the basic emotions, temptations, joys, sorrows and tribulations. They look back with proper perspective and in most cases they can be wonderfully helpful. Oh, of course, there are plenty of nitwits among adults too, but you will recognize and discount them.

To get back to the fear of making the wrong decision, just remember you won't be the first one to do it, and I still think it's better to make a poor decision than none at all. There is no contract binding you to your choice. If you've made a mistake, change it right away—as soon as you know for sure. And that's a decision too!

By the way, if one of your decisions is to go into the theater, please prepare for it. It is difficult for you, or anyone, to decide whether you have the talent for it when you begin unless you are gifted with singing and/or dancing ability and have been pushed by your family into being what is often scornfully called "a showoff."

Because I am always on the prowl for young talent and frequently need child performers, I am not a bit against doting mothers (it is almost always the mothers) who encourage their young to recite or sing or do the Twist for Auntie Jean, or whomever.

Of course some of these demonstrations are pretty embarrassing, but only when the child is unwilling, unhappy or self-conscious. However, I have had some positively thrilling moments too, when I have discovered self-confidence and real ability oozing from every six-year-old pore.

If you and your family are firmly convinced of your talent and you are truly serious about making the performing arts your career, then cram in all the training you can.

Talent and technique are absolute necessities today. A pretty face and/or figure will get you nowhere. Even the youngsters in off-Broadway shows are highly trained and infinitely capable. Broadway chorus people of today could have been soloists twenty years ago.

If it is the executive end of the theater you hanker for, by all means learn to typewrite. We use nonresident term girls from Bennington College as production assistants each season in our Light Opera Company office at City Center, and only good typists are given the opportunity. Good typists always seem to be a basic need in theatrical offices.

Whatever your aims for a career are, prepare now. What I have said about the theater is just as true if you are going into fashion, advertising, industry or journalism. The requirements for an academic career are already explicit.

As I said in the beginning, seventeen is a darling age. Savor it, enjoy it. Above all, make the most of it!

GLENN T. SEABORG

The Atom in Your Future

Glenn T. Seaborg has been chairman of the Atomic Energy Commission since 1961. His interest in science was first kindled in high school. In 1940 he became co-discoverer of element 94 (plutonium). In 1951 Dr. Seaborg was a co-winner of the Nobel Prize in chemistry, and eight years later he was awarded the Atomic Energy Commission's Enrico Fermi Award for his work in the field of nuclear chemistry and for his leadership in scientific and educational affairs. While serving as chancellor of the University of California at Berkeley, he was appointed to his current position by President John F. Kennedy.

Because your future is going to be quite a bit longer than mine, I think it is important that you should know some of the things which are being done today to promote the peaceful atom and to prevent the spread of nuclear weapons—in short, to use the atom to build a better world for you.

In the summer of 1964 I attended an international conference in which some three thousand men and women, delegates from about seventy-five nations, met in Geneva, Switzerland, to discuss the Atom—its many peaceful applications and its outlook for the future.

This was the *Third* International Conference on the Peaceful Uses of Atomic Energy and by far the most successful. As chairman of the United States delegation to that conference, I was impressed by the scope of the conference and by the enthusiasm of those attending. I was also impressed by a single thought which kept recurring to me during the ten days of meetings, discussions and exhibitions: Here was a meeting of people from many countries of the world drawn together to share their knowledge of the peaceful atom while at the same time, among many of these same countries, another aspect of the atom—its great destructive potential—was one of the things which divided them and prompted substantial distrust and fear. In fact, in that very city discussion was also taking place, and had been for some time, on disarmament and ways to reduce the tensions caused by the ever-present threat of a nuclear holocaust.

It is true that the atom presents two faces, but then so does almost every form of energy, every innovation and invention that man has ever adopted or applied throughout his history. Fire has both warmed us and burned us. The wind has driven our sailing ships and turned our windmills, but at times leveled our homes. Dynamite has been a boon to mining and excavation projects, but it also greatly increased the terror of war. Water has given us channels of transportation and sources of power, but it has also eroded our soil and flooded our cities. Tools and machines of all types and degrees of complexity have been used equally to save us labor and produce goods and as weapons of destruction. But man has learned, and is learning, how to control these elements of nature and tools of civilization and the purposes for which he uses them.

The atom is not good or evil in itself, but one thing is certain—its nuclear energy is by far the greatest, most versatile source of energy man has yet tapped. Therefore the uses to which we put it—beneficially or destructively —will have a tremendous effect on your future.   *100*

Let us look first at some of the many ways in which nuclear energy is being put to work. As you probably know, through the controlled fission of certain uranium atoms we are able to create enormous amounts of heat with a relatively small amount of nuclear fuel. This heat is safely produced in atomic furnaces called nuclear reactors. By various methods we use this heat to create large amounts of steam, which in turn is used to generate electricity, currently our most usable form of energy. Although we still have abundant sources of fossil fuels—coal, oil and gas—left in our earth, these irreplaceable resources are not going to last forever. Our rapidly growing demand for more and more electrical power, as our world population grows and industrializes, makes the development of nuclear power a necessity. We already have thirteen nuclear power plants, of many different types, at work in the United States. Safely and efficiently these plants are presently generating enough power to supply the needs of more than one million families. We are continuing to develop new plants with larger and more efficient types of reactors, those which will economically "burn" more of their nuclear fuel. Among these are plants which we refer to as "breeders," reactors which actually create more new fuel than they consume. The successful operation of such nuclear plants will assure the world of substantial amounts of fissionable fuel until such time as we may be able to harness the enormous power of controlled fusion and use as our fuel the almost limitless supply of heavy hydrogen found in common sea water. So you see, as far as power to light, heat and run your homes and cities is concerned, your atomic future is very bright. Nuclear power may also allow someday for new cities to be built where none could have existed before. We are now planning large-scale nuclear desalting plants which will provide arid areas with hundreds of millions of gallons of fresh water every day and at the same time supply electricity.

Nuclear propulsion for ships has proved highly successful, not only for submarines, but for cargo and passenger ships. Perhaps you have seen the sleek nuclear ship *Savannah,* the world's first atomic merchant ship. The N.S. *Savannah,* capable of sailing around the world fourteen times on a single fuel loading, has already made several trips to European and Pacific ports and has been welcomed and acclaimed in every one. Other nuclear ships are being planned and built, including some by Japan and Germany.

Looking further into the future, we are optimistic that nuclear propulsion will play a vital role in another type of transportation—space travel. Tests to date on our prototypes for nuclear rockets have been very successful. It will be these kinds of rockets which will propel the first spacemen to Mars and beyond, and perhaps take you or your children on such a journey.

All of you are aware of the enormous explosive power of the atomic and hydrogen bombs, but this same power can be put to tremendous constructive uses. The Atomic Energy Commission's Project Plowshare is conducting research and experiments which will permit us to safely use the atom's muscles for massive earth-moving tasks such as the digging of canals, the cutting of mountain passes and tunnels and the construction of major harbors where none existed before. The same nuclear power will be used underground in new forms of mining and to create subterranean storage areas.

Another form of nuclear energy, much different in nature and scope, is the radiation which comes from the unstable atoms we call "radioisotopes." The radioisotope, which has been called "the greatest scientific tool since the invention of the microscope," has proved invaluable in almost all branches of scientific and industrial research. It is being used today in medicine, agriculture and many types of industry to create a healthier, more abundant life for you. Each day new uses of the radioisotope are explored and adopted, and the promise of its future applications seems limited only by the imagination of man. *102*

Currently, a few of its uses are to preserve certain foods, diagnose and treat cancer, create a new and stronger type of wood, detect crime, develop healthier crops and power electronic equipment both at the bottom of the sea and far out in space. Quite an amazing bit of versatility, don't you think?

One final bow toward the peaceful atom before we turn to the other side of the picture. The atomic age has ushered in a new era of scientific research which has affected almost every branch of science. This research, much of it very basic, has broadened our horizons tremendously. It is bringing us much closer to the answers to questions men have been asking for thousands of years. What are we? Where did we come from? Where are we going? Nuclear energy and the nuclear sciences are propelling us on our long journey of discovery at a greater and greater rate. It will be an exciting journey.

Now I can hear many of you saying, "This is all very fine, but this future we can look forward to may be a very short one if a nuclear war should take place." You have need to be concerned over this, as every responsible member of society does. But though it is overshadowed by newspaper headlines on nuclear weapons, military alliances and the tensions of world politics, a considerable effort has been made, and continues to be made every day, to reverse the nuclear arms race and to encourage cooperation in controlling the materials which go into the production of weapons. Safeguards have been established which permit international inspection to prevent any nations receiving atomic materials for peaceful uses from converting them into weapons materials. Talks are continuing on plans to extend this inspection system. We are optimistic that they will succeed. The International Atomic Energy Agency (IAEA) is playing the key role in this international inspection with the cooperation of both the United States and the Soviet Union. The IAEA is an organization about which you will hear more and more.

The Limited Test Ban Treaty, which was signed by more

than one hundred nations during President Kennedy's and President Johnson's administrations, has also reduced the spread of weapons. By eliminating tests in the atmosphere it has reduced fallout today to a low level.

Much popular fiction today—books and movies—warns us of the possibilities of an "accidental" nuclear war. The chances of such a thing happening are more remote now than they have ever been. I can assure you that more thought and ingenuity have gone into safeguards against "accidents" than into the wildest of science fiction. Also you may be assured that your concern over the possibilities of a nuclear war is being shared by a great many people here and around the world, intelligent, dedicated people who are working hard to try to maintain peace and solve those problems which separate nations.

Finally, let me share with you one other thought which occurred to me at the recent Geneva Conference. Although there was some feeling of competition among the participants at the conference, the predominant feeling was one of good will and excitement in discovering and sharing new knowledge of the atom and the possibilities it offers in making a better world for all of us. If the peaceful atom could bring so many of us together to discuss and share common interests, and if we are willing to work together in using this new force for the common good, perhaps it will be the atom itself which will lead us away from its destructive face and toward a brighter and better tomorrow.

PETER SELLERS

The Gesture of Creation

Peter Sellers, England's brilliant comedian, discovered he had an ear for "voices" as a child when he mimicked accents at parties to approving laughter. He came by his love of show business naturally—his grandmother was a theatrical impresario. American movie fans "discovered" Peter in a wacky comedy, The Mouse That Roared, *in which he played three roles. Since then he has brightened films like* Dr. Strangelove, What's New Pussycat?, After the Fox *and* Casino Royale.

Most of my life I spend pretending to be somebody else. Possibly as a result, I often forget what I'm really like. This can be terrible at times, when it seems to me I don't have any personality of my own at all. No doubt this is something many actors experience, and not only actors. Consciously or unconsciously, I'm sure that many of us tend to mimic others in some way or other, to imitate qualities we rightly or wrongly admire. When I was at school I remember doing my best, at one stage, to model myself on a boy famous and popular on account of his modesty and firm character. But it's a confusing game. As an actor, I'm forever *pretending* to be somebody; as a man, I want to *be* somebody myself.

In other words I want to be as complete a person as

possible. People talk about "life." To me, life simply means living; and living means being somebody. I don't mean being a Big Man, with a couple of Cadillacs; I mean, as I've tried to explain, just being a person. I know I'm a terribly difficult person to live with, for the obvious reason that I'm so unsure of myself. (I should write it "my *self*.") If I can't really find a way to live with myself, I can't expect anyone else to live with me. I think our best friends are the people who make us sure of ourselves, sure of our ground. I've had a number of best friends who've been able to do this, but the confidence has worn off when they've gone.

I think we must all be conscious of some need for self-fulfillment. The trouble is it's the second part of that double-barreled cliché we think important. As a result we hunt around looking for the form fulfillment should take in our particular case. Unless we're very lucky and single-minded, and really know what it is we want and where we're going, this is a frustrating hunt. However, I think I've learned that the important bit is the first part of that cliché. It's ourselves we want to fulfill, to find. What we have to decide is what we ourselves should be. Nobody can tell us; nobody has a right. Wrong on a grand scale ensues when somebody tries to tell us. The inquisitor, the SS officer—they tried to tell us. The most important thing is tolerance. We must be ready to tolerate anything except intolerance, which is the greatest wrong; I think the other great wrongs are complacency and insincerity.

D. H. Lawrence and William Blake are, I think, the greatest moralists I have read, the men who have said the most valid things about life. Blake, who wrote: "The worship of God is honoring his gifts in other men"; Lawrence—misrepresented as the man who demonstrated the Original Apple, as grown in the Garden of Eden—who was British to the core, whose whole work was an affirmation of human values, the only important things, at a time when society and industry were increasingly denying their importance.

I believe, with Blake, that "everything living is holy." Blake also wrote that "Jesus Christ was all virtue, and acted from impulse, not from rules."

I reckon "impulse" means soul. Lawrence called soul "the *wholeness* of a man . . . the unknown him, as well as the known." A man's whole self, that's what we're looking for. Lawrence in fact was provoked to formulate a sort of creed of his own, in which he took up his ideas that man's soul is like a forest inhabited by various instincts and impulses. Blake puts it this way: "All deities reside in the human breast." Because I think there is so much truth in Lawrence's creed I will quote it in full. It goes:

This is what I believe:

That I am I.

That my soul is a dark forest.

That my known self will never be more than a little clearing in the forest.

That gods, strange gods, come forth from the forest into the clearing of my known self, and then go back.

That I must have the courage to let them come and go.

That I will never let mankind put anything over me, but that I will try always to recognize and submit to the gods in me and the gods in other men and women.*

Lawrence's summing up tells me a lot: "Either we are materialistic instruments . . . or we move in the gesture of creation, from our deepest self, usually unconscious. We are only the actors; we are never wholly the authors of our own deeds or works."

"We are only the actors. . . ." Acting is only a means

* From *Studies in Classic American Literature* by D. H. Lawrence. Copyright 1923, 1960 by Frieda Lawrence, © 1961 by the Estate of the late Mrs. Frieda Lawrence. Reprinted by permission of The Viking Press, Inc.

of existing; it isn't living itself. The actor starts with the blueprint of a character, a few written lines, a script. Using as much valid raw material—that is to say, life—as he can, he then builds up the character layer upon layer. He finishes by burying himself, or his self, underneath. This is a conscious and in part materialistic process. I have a certain confidence as an actor and very little as a person. I lack the faith in myself to let go of the side and swim: really to be somebody. When Lawrence says "creation," he means the creation of a whole person, not of *another* person, however apparently true to life. I lack the faith to make that gesture; maybe that's why I've got to be an actor.

ALICIA MARKOVA

A Dancer's Life

Alicia Markova, director of the Metropolitan Opera Ballet Company (and a few years ago its prima *ballerina), was born in England. She made her United States debut in 1938 at the same house, as Giselle with the Ballet Russe de Monte Carlo. She began her professional career with the Diaghilev Ballet in Europe, later became the first permanent ballerina of England's Old Vic–Sadler's Wells Ballet (today the Royal Ballet) and made many worldwide tours. Now retired from actual performance, she directs not only the Metropolitan Opera ballets but also the Metropolitan Opera Ballet Studio in its presentation of educational programs for New York metropolitan area schools.*

Most people think of a prima ballerina as someone remote from everyday life. In a way this is true, and it comes about quite simply. The early discipline of a dancer's life excludes many things which most young people take for granted, including hobbies such as swimming, riding and skating, and social activities in which people normally meet and mingle in their leisure.

Moreover, when I started my career, this discipline was a good deal stronger than it is today. At the age of fourteen, when I was chosen by Diaghilev to join his famous ballet company, I spent practically every hour off-stage under the close guardianship of a governess. When traveling, or in the hotels of Monte Carlo or Paris, my every move was supervised and chaperoned! In ballet class I was under even sterner control of another sort. My great teacher of this period, Maestro Enrico Cecchetti, was a master of lashing rebuke and would not hesitate to use a real live cane on the legs of his pupils if he saw a fault. This may sound incredible today, but it was in the tradition of the time, and it certainly produced some wonderful results. Many great dancers have had reason to thank Cecchetti for his ruthless determination to bring out their talents.

When, because of Diaghilev's death, his ballet company was dissolved and I had to build my career anew, I still lived in isolation from the general public to a great extent. This was by no means the isolation of wealth, for my finances were strictly limited; but it was a life lived largely in rehearsal and onstage. I went on occasional holidays but the ballet ruled my time almost completely. Of course I had travel opportunities that sound dazzling on the face of it—but actually those long grueling tours of the United States, Canada and Mexico during the war years gave me virtually no chance to explore the fabulous places I visited. Sometimes I barely had the chance to admire the view. So it went on, my devotion to ballet increasing, if anything, as the larger obligations of stardom came along. For we all know that ballet is a great art requiring devotion and self-discipline for twenty-four hours a day and is not to be confused with a job that usually occupies one from nine till five. Nevertheless, the ballerina, while she may seem to be living a life apart, is really, like any other artist, absorbing and using the material of everyday life to nourish her art.

In my book, *Giselle and I,* I explained that my first ambition was to become a doctor—a life which would have brought me into immediate contact with people and their needs. This particular ambition of mine was changed—but through the years I have tried to put my understanding of life and people into each role I have danced, whether a princess, a bird or a country maiden. Sometimes this has been done instinctively, sometimes as the result of a special experience or study which threw light on the character in question.

Ballet may seem to be a self-contained world, but it is by no means watertight, and my own horizons have widened in unforeseen ways. For instance, as a young dancer I never spoke in public at all. My chosen contact with people was from stage to audience, and here I could face any gathering, however large, and enjoy a close communion with them through the language of the dance. But when it came to words, I much preferred the limelight to fall on someone else. Then, with the growing influence of television, I often found myself "trapped" into interviews before audiences of millions instead of just one reporter in my dressing room. As time went on I was asked to do special television programs and had my own radio series on BBC in England. So somehow this idea of explaining the art of ballet in words began to snowball for me until today I lecture to audiences of thousands regularly and find the process quite natural.

However, this image of the young dancer living in a specialized world is of course still valid, though not quite, perhaps, in the way I experienced it. Dancers must lead disciplined lives because regular practice is essential to their function. In our schooling, bodies and minds must be trained from childhood in a unique way. No doubt the number of students who are potential ballerinas will always be limited; but many who long for the ballet can now approach it in other ways—through the sister arts of music or stage designing, or simply through a keen enjoyment of ballet performances.

When the famous impresario Sol Hurok first brought me to dance in the United States in the late 1930's on coast-to-coast tours with the Ballet Russe de Monte Carlo, there were tens of millions of Americans who had still never seen a ballet. The great Anna Pavlova had taken her company to remote towns across the length and breadth of the country, but the memory which she left behind was of something enchantingly foreign and fairy-like. The idea of a native American ballet company was still unborn.

Today the picture has changed completely. Ballet in America is now established with an honorable past and a very healthy future—with many regional and civic groups as outlets for the wealth of talented young Americans who are in training and inspired to dedicate themselves wholly to a great art.

ARTHUR J. GOLDBERG

Will You Be Ready?

HENRY GROSSMAN

Arthur J. Goldberg gave up his position as Justice of the United States Supreme Court in 1965 to become the Permanent Representative of the United States to the United Nations, with the rank of Ambassador. Before his Supreme Court appointment he had served as Secretary of Labor under the Kennedy administration. He began his career as a lawyer in Chicago and later served as counsel for the AFL-CIO, the United Steel Workers of America and other labor groups.

I accepted with pleasure the invitation of the editors of *SEVENTEEN* to write to you, for I know of no better way to judge the worth of our society as a whole than by the prospects it holds for the young. Perhaps the central truth about the future is that our lives are now committed to scientific progress in the economy and to the success of freedom throughout the world.

This two-fold commitment determines the direction of most American careers. What you become, the kinds of opportunity presented to you, the value you place upon your own labor and, ultimately, the worth of your contribution to our nation's strength and progress—*all* are determined by education and ability. Michelangelo's motto, "I am still learning," might well serve as the best practical advice anyone could give today.

The rhythm of occupational life has changed drastically. It used to be that a person's schooling was followed by some job shifting and then by an attachment to an industry, or a single firm, that would last his whole working life. Today, the educational period is open-ended; the need for study continues long after a diploma is awarded. A career may be broken frequently by shifts not only to different companies but to entirely different industries, some younger than the working person.

Against this background of change, employment prospects for the unskilled are vanishing, and the plight of the school dropout becomes even clearer. Young people who leave school when there is no need to are disqualifying themselves from a share of the future. A potential for learning and self-development which is cut short by early abandonment of education is not only an economic loss to the nation, it is also a profound personal tragedy.

Some seven and one-half million students are expected to leave school before graduation in this decade alone. Some will do so involuntarily—forced by personal circumstances to seek work earlier than they would choose.

But for them, and for all young people, I would like to reiterate my conviction that in the United States today education is nothing more than a matter of will.

Whoever genuinely desires an education can get one.

We hear a great deal of talk about the expense of education, and there is no question that costs have risen with improvements in facilities and more realistic pay scales. We hear less about an equally valid feature of education today—its availability. Working one's way through school is not easy, as I can testify personally. But today there are many scholarships, grants, special funds and tuition arrangements—not to mention job opportunities—available. There are also large numbers of local institutions such as junior colleges, extension services, special-hour courses that bring an education within the reach of any and all willing to work for it.

This abundance of educational opportunity contributes to the increase in productivity, which, in turn, advances living and working standards. And beyond that it makes equality of opportunity a great deal more than an abstract ideal. A technically oriented economy erases the old distinctions of sex and race and age—except where human conscience has failed to keep pace. Americans have been led by their own experience, for example, to a new regard for the contribution women make to economic life.

By far the largest number of women have traditionally been employed in offices as secretaries, in stores as salesgirls, in homes as domestic helpers and in schools as teachers.

But more and more women are finding work today in laboratories and research centers. The sciences are at the same time the field most often overlooked or disregarded by young women planning their careers—and the field where new careers are opening the fastest. Although only fifteen thousand women are today employed in the natural sciences, the pressing demand offers an unlimited opportunity for those who qualify. The young woman who selects her curriculum with the sciences in mind today is not likely to be disappointed in the future.

Most women today work because of necessity. Of every five women in the labor force, two either provide their own sole support or act as the heads of families. Most working women are from families with incomes under five thousand dollars per year. Yet there is a new element in women's working psychology, a new sense of opportunity to contribute to the making of a better society.

The old argument of "where a woman's place is" is futile in the light of today's brilliant opportunities—both in the home and in a career. I have never felt there was a natural hostility between the two. The woman who understands the world in which she and her children must live, who develops an interest and a competence in a field of work, also has the qualities of education and understanding that make her a good mother and homemaker. Most women today work before marriage and then re-enter the labor force after their families have been raised. The full opportunity to do both well is one of the advantages we are creating as a people.

One of the important aspects overlooked in discussions about working women is that a competitive economy, operated by a society in which millions are still poor and in need, can make full use of the compassion and sympathy that women bring to the rearing of their own families.

Finally, I want to say this: Being given a chance to learn and to work is one thing; the *reasons* for learning and working are another. If one's responses to life can be stated only in terms of position, status or accumulated wealth, then both the education and the labor are failures. It is, after all, man's spirit that is at stake in history. It is the greatest gift of all to be able to enrich it.

ROSALIND RUSSELL

Mothers, Pro and Con

Rosalind Russell, who has delighted audiences in more than forty-five movies, was born in Waterbury, Connecticut, one of seven children. After graduating from college, she studied acting at the American Academy of Dramatic Arts. Among her most popular films were Night Must Fall, My Sister Eileen *and* Picnic. *She was seen on Broadway as the famed* Auntie Mame, *and for her performance in the movie adaptation, she won her fourth Academy Award nomination. Having completed her role as Mrs. Rosepettle in the film of* Oh Dad, Poor Dad, *she plans to return to Broadway in* Coco. *Miss Russell is married to producer Frederick Brisson and has one son.*

Dear, dear teen-agers:
Thought I'd get a little note off to you from Jamaica. This glorious island is one of the few places I've seen that outdoes the postcards. I'm here making a film called *Oh Dad, Poor Dad, Mama's Hung You in the Closet and I'm Feelin' So Sad.* The title is almost as long as the script. It's Sunday, my day off. I got to thinking about you while I was studying the scene that Bobby Morse (who plays my son) and I are going to do tomorrow.

You see, this story is about Momism . . . yes, and Dadism too. Those two people around your house who keep bugging you.

This Mom I'm playing is a terror: the Mom to end all Moms. I admit her type does exist. She is, however, the exception and that is why I am writing you.

I know some of you are members of the Anti-Mom Army. (Were you drafted or did you enlist?) I happen to be in the other camp. I'm a Mom and we also have a number of recruits. You may say, "Yeah, *too* many!" If you are one who does, please read my letter twice.

Now, this parents' outfit I'm part of is anxious to make contact with your group. To put it delicately, we'd like a peek now and then into your compound. We don't know whether to knock on the door or break it down. It would be great if you would open it a crack or maybe peer over the top. We really don't want to fight you. We just want to wave . . . to cheer you on . . . to wish you well in all your battles.

Though you are well organized now, you must remember a few years ago when you were young, that feeling of being alone, of being on the outside looking in. That's the way we adults often feel, and the older you are the more acute the loneliness.

You may think we want to snoop. We don't. And you know why? Because we had a setup just like yours a while back. We used your own tactics on our parents. The only difference is that we let the old folks into our club now and then. Or maybe they sneaked in. But I am leveling with you when I tell you they behaved very nicely. I noticed right away that they laughed a lot. I thought then it was because they were delighted to be there, but after the third or fourth "visit," I discovered these characters actually had a sense of humor. Now, don't get all shook up at this "message." Keep an eye out. I mean, keep an eye open.

For instance: My best friend in my teens, Ellen Crammer, had a mother who laughed at anything . . . a card. We were practicing smoke rings in the attic one rainy afternoon when we heard her explode with laughter. It seemed a good time to ask for extra cash, so we popped the coffee beans in and went down to investigate. There was Ellen's footlocker just arrived home from summer camp. Mrs. Crammer was holding several white bath towels, all spanking new save one. The one didn't look much like a towel . . . it wasn't gray and it wasn't black. It was somewhere in between, and as Ellen pointed out, you could still read the name tape.

"So what if I didn't take a bath for eight weeks? Three times a day in that lake was enough."

Mrs. Crammer was hysterical as she put those towels away in the linen closet. We didn't dig it then. But twenty years later I had the same laugh when my son's footlocker came back from prep school.

Looking back, I remember that the ole folks not only laughed it up, they came in handy in a pinch. I had a boy friend then. His name was Wheaton . . . his first name yet. He was slightly wall-eyed, but he had a car. Well, it wasn't exactly a car, but it had four wheels, no doors, a klaxon horn, isinglass curtains and two scalloped running boards. We were going from Waterbury, Connecticut, all the way to New York to the final game of the World Series. My old man forfeited his tickets on my sworn statement that I'd stop tearing up my report cards.

Wheaton cranked his car for an hour and a half before he went into the house and woke up his father. The old boy swore a lot but he sure knew the innards of that Stutz Bearcat. You should have seen his pajamas by the time we took off. True, ye moms and dads ask a lot of questions . . . they are mighty curious, and, being old, they talk up a storm and repeat themselves. They keep reminiscing with those standards: "When I was your age" and "You don't understand but you will when you grow up"—all that dull stuff.

But we learned to ride with the punch and found most of them to be good eggs. Yeah, that was a phrase we used then. Like "So's your old man" . . . "Says you."

Our entire first division were experts in pig Latin. Corny. Still, you have some dillies of your own: "You're a gas" . . . "That's real boss" . . . and that "flake out" bit always reminds me of pie. Well, let's not go into that.

Back to the anti-mom and -dad camp. How about meeting us parents twice a week? All right, *once* a week . . . on a neutral ground? We'll bring the food as usual and you can bring your laundry as usual, including those rigid sweat socks.

You'll know us by the pride in our eyes and by our outstretched arms. No, we won't smother you. We promise. We want to stand by you, not *over* you. We want to talk with you, not to dictate to you. We want to talk frankly, not nag you. We want to discipline you because we're supposed to. We want your cooperation to help us be better parents.

We want your respect, and most of us know we must earn that respect. We want you to forgive our mistakes or at least try to overlook them.

Above all, we want to love you, and you cannot deny us this because we loved you *first*.

Well, I'd better sign off now before this becomes a "lecture." I've got to hit the sack anyway because I have an early call on the set.

Take care of your very special and precious selves. You're all we've got . . . our hope and our real joy. Check in now and then by phone or smoke signal . . . but *check!* It's comforting to know you're not a spot on the freeway. The price of dye for gray hair keeps escalating. Get it? Supply and demand.

Write when you get there. You don't need to wait till you get work.

Love and some of those boring kisses too,

Mom Rosalind Russell Rosepettle

CHET HUNTLEY

The Sound of Beauty

Chet Huntley, one of television's outstanding news commentators, has been listening to himself as well as others for many years, ever since he dropped his pre-med major after winning a collegiate national oratory tournament in 1932. He can be heard weekday nights sharing the Huntley-Brinkley Report *and on various news specials.*

MY wife has approved this . . . with a bit of hesitation; but it is our considered judgment that I might as well come clean, confess, and acknowledge publicly that I am harboring a persistent, nagging and irrepressible crush on Gladys. Perhaps an honest recognition of this trauma will cause it to ease and then go away.

It is not necessary, I should think, to identify Gladys. I have a sneaking suspicion that my passion for this contemporary Aphrodite is no isolated phenomenon. I am sure she is the *femme fatale* of a list of guys as endless as the Manhattan telephone directory. But I have a notion that *my* affection for Gladys is founded on something different from that of the others. In any event, I suspect I am unique in that I have analyzed what the charm of Gladys really is.

She does, indeed, catch and delight the eye; but what

is it that makes her different? What is it that sets her apart?

Gladys has ear appeal!

Her voice is like the liquid throatings of a muted guitar. It contains, at once, the soulful vibrations of an *E* string and the gossamer laughter of high *C*. The basic contralto richness is flecked with lyric and mezzo-soprano grace notes in ratios dependent upon her mood and the subject of her talk.

But that is not all! Gladys glorifies an occasional word or a rare inflection with melodic lilt containing a minute suggestion of her ancestral Catalonia.

Gladys is a talking love-theme played by Pablo Casals!

I remember a particularly beautiful stewardess on a flight out of London one night. She had been generously endowed with every feature to qualify as an exceptionally lovely young woman. Then, as we poised on the runway for the long flight over the polar route to San Francisco, she spoke into the public-address system to welcome us aboard. The effect was as rude and abrupt as if she had suddenly revealed a bald head. How could such a gloriously contrived masterpiece of feminine construction be the source of those pinched and wispy sounds? In an instant, that girl had been reduced from a breath-taking beauty to the crowded ranks of the commonplace. And at the risk of confessing to a galloping inconstancy, I must also cite my abiding yen for Betsy Palmer. The combination of her voice and diction, emanating from that lovely mouth, has the features of a sunburst. Betsy has glorified South Chicagoese. How she did it I have not the foggiest notion, but look what happened to Liza Doolittle! I could sit and listen to Betsy reading the dictionary. The most perfect and beautiful English in the world, believe it or not, is not spoken in England, no matter what my English friends will say. Beautiful English is a product of Dublin and Cork. I have long believed that the purity and beauty of their spoken English explains much of the success of the several Irish theater companies. They make things happen to this language of ours. They rescue it from the wreckage we make of it and transform it into a thing of delight: musical, melodic and rich with all the nuances of subtle expression. You leave the theater congratulating yourself on "almost speaking the same tongue."

There is a little verse which every child of Cork or Dublin knows and which goes like this:

> With deep affection
> And recollection
> I often think of
> Those Shandon Bells
> Whose sounds so wild would,
> In the days of childhood,
> Fling round my cradle
> Their magic spells.
> On this I ponder
> Where ere I wander
> And thus grow fonder,
> Sweet Cork, of thee;
> With thy Bells of Shandon
> That sound so grand
> On the pleasant waters
> Of the River Lee.

It is not a masterpiece of poetry, particularly, as you or I read it aloud, but ask an Irishman from Cork or Dublin to recite it and that little verse becomes a wondrous and delightful audio jewel. The *l* and double *l* sounds are placed on the tip of the tongue and at the forward section of the roof of the mouth. The result is that this sound, which occurs so frequently in our language, is transformed from a nondescript gargle into the melody of a waterfall of honey. The "ink" sound, as the Irish manage it, becomes one of the most pleasant of the language: forward against the teeth and tinkling like ice crystals. The vowel sounds are used to their full potential. They are the whole notes of our language . . . places

where the violinist would draw from his instrument those

great prolonged sounds of sorrow, ecstasy, sadness and happiness. Consider the word "music." It is one of the finest words in any language, for it can convey its meaning by sound alone. Ordinarily we give it no opportunity, but an Irishman will make it sing.

Beautiful speech is not difficult to acquire. A single school year of instruction is sufficient to master the sounds and the rules which govern them. From then on it is merely a matter of reading aloud and applying the rules. By the way, reading aloud in correct speech is actually just as entertaining and satisfying as playing a stack of your favorite phonograph records. Voice quality, too, can be altered or changed with no great effort. The human larynx is an incredible instrument. It will do just about anything the brain tells it or demands of it. Upon request, and with a bit of practice, the human sound system will overhaul itself and become a thing of rare beauty.

The American girl is aware of most of the ingredients of beauty: posture, coiffure, make-up, costume and the rest. But she frequently quite overlooks voice and diction. Through all her years, a woman will depend mainly upon her speech to communicate to others her convictions, her feelings, her hopes and fears. Virtually all that she is or hopes to be will be expressed in speech. Is it not obvious, then, that her speech should be attractive? It can be her crowning glory. To be beautiful, a girl must sound so.

Moreover, if the American girl will undertake the beautification of our language—this noble and ancient tongue—the boys will soon follow suit. We men are a bit too timid to lead the way.

BENNY GOODMAN

The Brave Teen Years

Benny Goodman, the King of Swing, plays a mighty clarinet. Born in Chicago, he makes music heard around the world—from the purest kind of jazz to the absolute precision of Mozart and Brahms. While his international tours (including a one-week stand with his orchestra at the 1958 World's Fair in Brussels) have firmly established him as a potent goodwill ambasador, his recordings continue to delight enthusiasts at home. Classic albums include Carnegie Hall Jazz Concert *for Columbia and* The Golden Age of Swing *for RCA Victor.*

Granted that all America, and for all I know the world, has come to recognize teens as a world apart. Granted also that teens now have their special literature, fashions, even specialized advertising appeal. Despite all of these undeniable evidences of new stature for teens, there's one more evidence I'd like to see as further proof that young people really do merit all the attention and emphasis the adult world is lavishing on them.

I'd like to see the teens themselves realize they're more than an age, more than a population group. They're the sole owners and directors of a precious span of life that lasts a meager seven years. A span during which, it seems to me, they have the opportunity to lay the groundwork through brave living for the full, rich life.

The teen years are a time of life when financial security isn't of paramount importance. Life is ahead for the making of a fortune. So the teen-ager can afford to be brave, even aggressive, in making the most of his abilities and talents. He can afford to ask—and not be afraid of a rebuff. I remember at the age of thirteen getting professional playing jobs and demanding to be and getting paid. In my early teen years I didn't hesitate to apply for jobs to big-name band leaders, theater owners, anyone and everyone who could give me work. And I got work, too.

I'm living proof that being poor is not a handicap. In a way, not having enough can and should be a prod to the teen-ager to be brave enough to go out and earn what he lacks. Scarcely a week passes that my mail doesn't contain wonderful letters from teen-agers telling how they work to pay for music lessons; how they get up at dawn to have time to practice before leaving for school. These are brave kids in my book. They're making the most of teen strength and singleness of purpose.

Back in the crazy twenties and depressed thirties it wasn't very fashionable to admit to serious thinking on important topics if you were very young. In fact I recall a sort of fear among teen-agers that if they admitted to deep thinking they'd be out of it socially. But I notice today that there seems to be a complete lack of this kind of fear. Teen-agers today seem to have a keen awareness of the national economy, international politics, world problems. I notice this characteristic in my own children, Rachel and Benjie, and in their friends. It's exciting to listen to them—especially when I remember that today's teen-agers are tomorrow's leaders. What with the mad pace of life today giving us a foretaste of what the pace will be in the years ahead, we'll surely be needing extra-special leaders in the future.

Talking about serious subjects—I'd like to emphasize one now. Strictly from my own experience, I know that a whole new and wonderful world can open up to the person brave enough to stop, take personal inventory and humbly admit that a new start is in the cards. If you think it doesn't take courage, just try it. And the younger you are when you do it, the easier it is. It happened to me back in 1949. I suppose I should have been content: records selling in the millions, concerts SRO. Presumably I had everything a man could want—professionally and in private life. But the one thing I didn't have was the personal satisfaction of knowing I was playing the old clarinet as well as it could be played. I was forty years old. It was time for a stop and an inventory and a decision.

I had then been playing many soloist engagements with symphony orchestras and chamber music groups and decided to learn a new way to play this particular kind of music.

I'd been taught to hold the mouthpiece between my front teeth and lower lip—another system was to use only the lips. Well, I simply had to start from scratch and learn to double-lip and acquire a different fingering technique. I don't mind admitting it isn't easy at age forty, as it is at age eighteen, to be brave enough to start over. But it changed my whole life and career. I acquired a more controlled technique. Whatever hesitancy I'd had about playing with symphony orchestras evaporated.

What I'm saying is this: if I could do it you teen-agers can do it. All it takes, really, is the courage to admit you're not so good as you can be—and the best time for such an admission is the teen years, while the future lies ahead.

My life with teen-agers is always in a crowd, listening or dancing. Of late, I've often wondered if the tremendous resurgence of interest in jazz is because it's one of the few uncomplicated pleasures left today. Sometimes, looking over the seas of young faces, I wonder if teen-agers ever take the time to be alone, if they realize the importance of being alone some of the time.

I know it's easier to be with a crowd. But if teen-agers would just have the bravery to make a point of taking time to be alone, they'd discover that being alone is a sort of self-renewal. I get it when I'm fishing. I get it when I'm practicing. Everyone needs to be alone, deliberately and premeditatedly alone, at times.

One of the things I've noticed in today's young people is the way they accept their world without any resentment. None of that chip-on-the-shoulder-look-what-a-mess-you-left-me-to-live-with kind of resentment of the twenties following World War I. Youth of today seems to take it in stride, and even at the risk of inviting letters from parents wondering where I've been hiding these past few years, I'll go out on a limb and say teen-agers of today are a more responsible lot than the world has seen in previous generations!

Looking back over the years it seems to me that by contrast, our teen-agers today are not only more responsible, they think in bigger terms. Where the youth of other generations saved for a suit or a dress, or for tickets for a show, the teens of today save for their own cars, for trips across country or abroad, for all sorts of costly extracurricular instruction. Everything for today's youth is so much more expensive than it was for us oldsters at their age; it's small wonder they've been forced to think "large."

My mail is a bottomless source of knowledge and understanding of today's youth—at least it is to me. I get letters from kids who married much too young. But they're not whining. They tell me their problems; they tell me what my music means to them; they talk about their dreams and their hopes, their varied paths to realization. But they don't whine. To me that's their bravery—and I, for one, give it my deepest respect.

I get letters from teen-agers who want advice on careers

in music. Many, many tell me their families are economically comfortable, but "I'm working after school and weekends to pay for my lessons." "After all," they explain, "with all the expenses my parents have putting the other kids through school, I don't want to saddle them with the burden of financing my career." Maybe, thinking it over, I should change the title of this piece from "The Brave Teen Years" to "Those Wonderful Teen-agers."

DAVID SARNOFF

The Promise of the Future

David Sarnoff, chairman of the board of the Radio Corporation of America, is a pioneer in the development of radio, TV and electronics. As head of RCA he is in charge of a vast corporation which, among other things, owns the National Broadcasting Company, and whose manufactures range from tiny ferrite cores for computers to huge radars used in tracking missiles and satellites. Born in Russia in 1891, he was brought to the United States in 1900; he began work selling newspapers and as a delivery boy; by the age of fifteen he had become a messenger for a cable company, soon saved enough money to buy a telegraph instrument and then learned the Morse Code. That was only the beginning of a distinguished career.

When I look back over half a century to the days before I was twenty, the perspective of the years sharpens my recollections of youthful dreams in an America verging upon a brilliant new age born of science and the inventions of Edison, Marconi, the Wright brothers and Lee de Forest. Then cosmetics were frowned upon for young ladies, and "teen-ager" was a term yet to be conceived. I was seventeen when laboratory experiments confirmed the suspected electronic character of electricity, and science was building the foundation of modern atomic physics. Even earlier, I had been brought directly into contact with an exciting technology so new that it had not yet been identified by the name of electronics. I was working as a messenger in the New York offices of the Marconi Wireless Telegraph Company of America, and there I had my first meeting with Marconi himself. It was an overwhelming occasion. I volunteered to run personal errands for him in my spare time, and I felt honored when he allowed me to do so.

You all know, of course, how science and technology have transformed our world since the days when I was a teen-ager. There has been more material progress as a result of scientific discovery and application since 1900 than in all the prior millenniums of recorded history. Of all scientists who have ever lived, ninety percent are alive and at work today. Yet even so, there are not enough scientists and engineers to assure our ability to grow and to master the competitive challenges and responsibilities of what we call the Space Age.

Unfortunately, few realize that a career in science must begin in high school. Unless a high school student takes science subjects and takes them seriously, he or she will not be ready for a science curriculum in college. Largely because of this, our colleges and universities no longer graduate enough technically qualified young men and women to meet our requirements for even greater numbers of scientists and engineers. The problem is made more urgent by the alarming fact, reported by the National Science Foundation, that the Soviet Union annually produces more science and engineering graduates than the United States. Edison went to work as a newsboy at the age of ten and became a telegraph operator at fifteen. I would not recommend a similar course to an aspiring scientist or engineer today—and neither would Edison, I am sure. Science has moved too far. Just *how* far was vividly brought home to me the day Colonel John Glenn went into orbit. I was traveling on the train from New

York for a meeting in Washington with President Kennedy. While I walked from my train seat to the dining car, Colonel Glenn flew a distance of 2,500 miles—from the Hawaiian Islands to the Pacific Coast. In the time it took me to travel from my home to Washington, Colonel Glenn flew 81,000 miles in space at a speed of 17,500 miles an hour. And I was tuned in on virtually every minute of his flight by home television, car radio, pocket radio on the train and hotel television. Not even the most imaginative science-fiction writers could have depicted this reality sixty years ago, when my own career began.

Young women of America represent our largest reservoir of potential scientific "manpower." Millions of women work today. Many thousands play significant roles in education and in business, and some are making important contributions to science. But unfortunately only three percent of the nation's 25,000 physicists today are women.

How can we interest you young people in considering careers in the field of science?

My own career has been influenced and inspired by the contacts which I have had with men of science. I did not have the opportunity to receive scientific training—or even a high school education. But I was fortunate enough to become acquainted in my early teens with the world of science and engineering through acquaintance with Marconi, and subsequently with a number of the outstanding scientists, engineers and inventors who were to create much of today's electronic technology. Through these personal contacts I caught some of the excitement and challenge of science and was led to apply myself to its advancement in whatever way I could.

This has convinced me that nobody is better qualified to stimulate the interest of youth in science than the working scientist himself. If only five percent of the more than 1,350,000 physical scientists and engineers in the United States were to devote a few days each year to education, our high school students would have direct access to nearly 70,000 of the finest technical brains.

Space flight, astrophysics, communications satellites, computers, rockets, lasers, nuclear physics, electron tubes, microelectronics, television, cryogenics and a host of other fascinating new specializations would come alive in your high school classroom through the person of the individual scientist or engineer, fresh from the workshops of the Space Age—the laboratory and the testing chamber. Regular classroom instruction would be enriched, and many more young people would become aware of the opportunities in science.

Most of the nation's scientists and engineers, of course, are in private industry—scattered in laboratory and plant locations from coast to coast. Would they be willing to contribute some of their precious time and knowledge to you, the high school student? I am convinced they would welcome the chance—if it were presented by educators and by private industry.

Consequently, I proposed a teaching program aimed at bringing the working scientist into the high school classroom, as a cooperative endeavor of private industry and our schools.

In the fall of 1962, such a program was launched by the Board of Education of the City of New York and the Radio Corporation of America. This pilot project ran through the 1962-63 school year at no cost to the school board, with the participation of fifteen top RCA scientists and engineers—including a young woman, Harriet Bein, who lectured on computers and data processing.

The results were encouraging and impressive. Of the students who participated, 89 percent said they wanted more class sessions given by working scientists, and 87 percent said these sessions would influence them toward careers in science. These responses were especially meaningful because the majority of participating students of both sexes had not previously specialized in science either at school or with home hobbies.

The frequently overworked high school science teacher proved to be the key to the success of the program. His or her awareness of the relevance and meaning of the subject matter to be discussed by a scientist made it possible to prepare students for the classroom session through homework assignments and special classroom activities.

In addition, only the teacher could advise the scientist on how best to attune his lecture to the students' actual level of understanding. In brief, a scientist's classroom session was successful only to the extent that it assisted the teacher.

The RCA scientists were also stimulated by the students. One scientist told me that he had been bombarded by questions so penetrating and pertinent that they might have come from his own laboratory assistants. I was not surprised, for the greatest appeal of science is its challenge to the curiosity of people of all ages. You don't have to be a genius to be a scientist, Marconi once told me; but you do have to be fascinated by the *why* of things.

After the practical value of the industry-science teaching program was affirmed, in September, 1963, the pilot program was expanded in New York with the additional participation of scientists from eight other companies. Now it is my fervent hope that private industry will enroll its scientists and engineers in similar cooperative projects in communities from coast to coast.

Tomorrow's scientists will find the potential to eliminate hunger, prolong health and mental vigor, control and destroy cancer as a mass killer, build electronic "spare parts" for the human body, perfect lasers to replace the mechanical instruments of surgery, harness nuclear power for economical home and individual use, establish interplanetary travel and existence as a way of life and make person-to-person intercontinental and interplanetary television contact a matter as routine as today's phone call.

Tomorrow's engineers will cooperate intimately with the scientists to translate the increasingly abstract and sophisticated language of science into devices that will benefit mankind.

How much will tomorrow's scientists and engineers achieve by the year 2000?

There will be many specific answers to that question. Most of them are locked, as they always have been, in the dreams of young men and women with the intelligence and determination to build a better and happier world.

If experience serves as a guide, the scientific achievements of the future will exceed the expectations of tomorrow's scientists and engineers, just as those of the past have exceeded the expectations of the Edisons, Wrights, Curies, Marconis and Einsteins. And—*yes*—many of tomorrow's science pioneers will be women.

PEARL S. BUCK

The Pursuit of Happiness

CLARA E. SIPPRELL

Pearl S. Buck, author of some fifty-eight books—fiction and nonfiction, for adults and for children—was the first American woman to win a Nobel Prize, in 1938. She is also a Pulitzer Prize winner for what is still perhaps her best-loved book, The Good Earth. *Her recent books include the novels* The Living Reed *and* Death in the Castle *and the nonfiction* Children for Adoption.

I have had and am still having a happy life. I think it is important to be happy. Life is not worth living when one is unhappy. That I learned long ago. The thing I had to learn was how to be happy. Yes, I had to learn it. It is really quite easy to be unhappy. The small details of daily life going awry can create such discontent that happiness is impossible. Then come the crashing disasters which overtake all of us, sooner or later, and life is unendurable. Worst of all, perhaps, the unhappiness may come out of discontent with ourselves, the way we look, the lack of talent and the environment in which we find ourselves. How then shall we escape the inescapable?

First let me say that the most important lesson life has taught me is that happiness, or even contentment, has to be planned for and worked for if it is to be achieved. No one on earth or in heaven has promised happiness or even contentment to any of us. We are born without promises. We find ourselves here, enclosed in a body which was not of our making and which may be very different from the one we would like to have had, and belonging to a group of persons called a family which may or may not be to our liking either. Yet each of us has certain talents and potentials for happiness and each of us is given the instrument by which we may put them to use. This instrument is the will. Some people use this instrument well and they find contentment and consequent happiness of a very permanent sort. Others never use the instrument and their lives sink into an habitual discontent, which can only result in permanent unhappiness.

What directs the will? It does not work alone. It is only an instrument. Well, the mind directs the will. The mind says, "This must be done, if happiness is to follow." For the will is a laggard. It likes to sleep. It prefers not to exert itself unless forced. So mind must force. Mind says, "I know this is what I must do, because it is what I want to do for my own contentment." Will is what makes you get up in the morning when mind says there is work to be done. It is so easy to change night into day by sitting up all hours doing nothing much. Then day changes into night, and nothing at all gets done. Discontent and unhappiness follow, since it is essential for the human creature to do and to be. Mind, then, is the planner, and will is the performer.

And in what area will the mind plan for contentment and for happiness? Let me recommend, from my own experience, that it be in the area of the arts—in music, in painting, in writing, in sculpture, in dance; the range is infinite. You will ask, is this not simply saying that one must have a hobby? No, I do not mean a hobby. Ideally one should decide what one likes best to do and then train the self to earn a living in that field. But this is not always possible. Sometimes talent is insufficient for earning a living and yet enough to provide for happiness. It is then worth the effort of pursuit. You will enjoy art more

138

if you pursue it without thought of money. Pursue it for pleasure, for release, for enrichment of the mind and spirit, for simple happiness. You will find that contentment follows. The tasks of daily life then are not so dreary, sorrow is lightened, loneliness becomes endurable.

Of course you must work. The will of the artist is his means of achievement, his energy. He soon learns that if he does not work, if he fills his time idly, he will be discontented and unhappy. And he is subject to all the temptations of the ordinary human being. Do I not know all too well how my own lazy will tries to deceive me? Even after many years I can still think of a dozen ways not to sit down to my typewriter in the morning. The will needs a whip sometimes to get it started, and the mind must provide the whip. "No," mind must insist, "the flowers cannot be watered now, nor the newspaper read, nor that telephone call made, nor anything else done except work." When the will cannot escape, it performs, and when it performs, mind has to work too. It is a curious interrelationship, this between mind and will. Mind decides for the will, and will gets to work upon mind. Long ago I learned that writing, for example, cannot depend upon the mood of the mind. Will sets mood aside and works upon mind, and mind, often reluctant at first, learns the habit of work. If mood is the ruler, then both will and mind fall into habits of lazy decay.

I know how difficult it is to understand the relationship of mind and will, especially at the beginning of learning an art. There is a certain amount of drudgery in every art. One cannot, for example, play the simplest piece of music without practice. But what joy when even the simple piece is mastered and can really be played! I recommend music, hopefully begun with a teacher, for art is most enjoyable when it is based upon accurate knowledge, even though performance never goes beyond the primary stage. There is also sculpture, a supremely satisfying form of art, employing hands as well as mind and spirit. When my children were small and my life was overcrowded with daily duties, I found rest and release in modeling their heads in clay or plaster. I caught them on the wing as they played, and though the heads were far from perfect from a professional point of view, they were likenesses. I look at them with tender memory, now that the children are grown men and women. But why should I enumerate the arts? Art is various and always new.

What I am saying, in brief, is that the pursuit of art through some chosen form, planned for and achieved by determination and persistence, brings permanent contentment and the illumination of genuine happiness to the human spirit. Life is never dull, the creature is never bored, when he—or she—becomes the creator.

ROD SERLING

Will the Real Dutch Uncle Please Stand Up?

Rod Sterling, creator of the TV science-fiction series Twilight Zone, *was born in Syracuse, New York. He broke in as a writer doing radio scripts in 1948, and switched to TV a few years later. Particularly notable were some of his* Playhouse 90 *dramas, like* Requiem for a Heavyweight. *His screenplay credits include* Patterns, Seven Days in May, *and* Assault on a Queen. *His most recent TV series was a western called* The Loner.

I am no longer, sad to say, a teen-ager. I departed that fraternity some years ago, leaving in a welter of Glenn Miller records, the Big Apple dance step, an oversized high school football jersey and an item of some worldwide consequence generically referred to as "Pearl Harbor." This is by way of establishing to the reader that this writer is an aging forty-year-old who admittedly did all of his growing up in another era. Considering the nature of *this* era, I've no doubt but that you youngsters have had your fill of adult Dutch Uncling. I know for a fact that you are berated, pushed, shoved, warned, restrained, apprised, exhorted and admonished until you must wonder, if adults have so much wisdom, why is this not the best of all possible worlds?

It is an incontestable fact that the generation of your

mothers and fathers (and of Rod Serling) was considerably less tension-ridden and far simpler. When I studied geometry and wore saddle shoes, there was no such thing as a hydrogen bomb. A bomb shelter hadn't been built yet this side of the Atlantic.

You young people, unfortunately, are forced into considerably more awareness of world problems as they exist today, because the earth has shrunk to about the size of the wing length of a supersonic bomber, and sounds are now distinct and easily heard across the earth—be they rifle shot or underground bomb test. In this respect a maturity is being forced upon you at a much earlier age than was our wont. The contrasts and dissimilarities are certainly evident, but there *are* problems quite universal and not specifically hooked to any given year *or* era. I list them now and make comment upon them only because I possess two things that you don't. One is a collection of years and the other is the *perspective* that comes with those years.

First and most important, don't let any adult deprecate or minimize your problems, your deep concerns or your frustrations. Whether it be unpopularity, a case of nerves, the passing misery of acne or a bum report card, they're real problems. They're to be suffered and sweated out and must be judged strictly in the context of how they affect you at the moment—not sloughed off because they're a phase of growing up and will depart the premises after the purchase of the first brassiere or the first real barbered shave. Only the Lord knows how many adults are forced into psychoanalysis at age thirty-five because of sweeping a problem under the rug at age twelve or thirteen. Your social problems are probably most with you at the moment, and it follows that this particular area has the most complications. No young adult—boy or girl—can help but hope to be popular. Part of popularity is a sense of belonging, of being part of a group, and in a sense, a conformance to whatever is the going average. The thing to remember here is that there is a price for popularity and sometimes that price comes too high. A high school girl dates a boy with a jazzed-up hot rod. This is a guy who drives as though his life depended on it and too often the few seconds he has saved by speed, he hasn't survived to find use of. Now it's a status symbol to date a popular boy, I'm sure. And I'm not too old to remember that an improvised drag race can be an important part of the scene. But if your common sense, as well as your own instincts for simple safety, happens to compete with popularity, you're a long country mile better advised to sacrifice status *and* popularity, even if it means having to turn down a date with somebody in a souped-up, very chic sports car. It figures that there'll be some accusations of "square" thrown at you. You may lose the friendship of the sixteen-year-old would-be jet pilot who has asked to squire you. But over the long haul, you'll be respected for having a point of view and a legitimate respect for your own well-being.

Nobody can tell you not to go steady because no human being has yet reached that point of sheer perfection when he can dictate what a heart feels, what a set of emotions orders or what your eyeballs feast on and decide they like. The thing to remember here is that you must take your affairs of the heart slow and easy. Since the beginning of man, it has been expected and it is also right and proper that two young people single each other out for special mutual attention and equally mutual attraction. There is nothing unsavory or unwholesome about this. My guess is that "going steady" is no phenomenon this year nor will it be a hundred years hence. And if it's the sort of thing that appeals to you, remember only one thing—that in ninety-nine cases out of a round one hundred, you'll have another romantic interest with the next change of season. Make your commitments temporary, even if you make the commitments. Don't limit yourself or your partner for the future because the dictates of the moment press the commitment. There will be other moments and other dictates and they'll come with just as much love and just as much sweet anguish as they do now.

You've got the nerves? Wanderlust? Funny little hungers that dig into you but defy understanding? Do you want and yet can't bespeak what it is you want? Don't let this indefinable frustration rack you up. This is neither unusual nor a mark of Cain. I can remember, as a fifteen-year-old, packing a suitcase once a week for a period of six months, deciding I'd go to sea or lie about my age and join the Army or get on a train to Canada. Yours is the age of the itchy feet and the itchy brain. It's reaching out now and it's growing. It's beginning to take on the preliminary form of adulthood. Don't succumb to this itch, but don't deny it either. Sit down with someone you love and respect and ask him (or her) how *he* handled it when the particular formless bug bit him. If your confidant is worth his salt, he'll probably tell you that there is a prescription you can take compounded of thought, reason, self-questioning, laughter and love. It won't solve your problems, whatever they are—but you'll be able to live with those problems and function despite them.

In looking back over my span of forty years, I think I've learned one basic thing. This is simply that you never stop learning. Somehow, some way, by a combination of observation, osmosis, books, conversation and the simple process of living, you take on dimension and breadth just by being alive and opening both your mind and your heart to the world around you.

And there are timeless, unchanging things of value that you must always respect. You can start learning that respect now. Believe in truth. Never lie to yourself or anyone else. Believe in that formless, amorphous thing called honor. Once it's possessed, you'll never cease having peace of mind. Believe in courage, even when courage is an uncomfortable, heavy weight thrust on your shoulders at an inopportune moment. The world you're stepping out into is no garden, but much of the weeding, the planting and the nurturing of growing things will be your job. And it's obviously the kind of job that will take courage. And lastly, believe in your fellow man. Believe in his worth and his dignity. Accept no one because of his wallet, his lineage or his color. Accept or reject because of what you read on his lips, the thoughts he conveys from his mind and the fact that he can evoke your love and respect.

We full-grown adults now moving downhill in the calendar of human events ask a great deal of you. We ask you to inherit a world which we've botched up miserably. We ask you to show the restraint which we, unhappily enough, have never exercised ourselves. We require of you a morality, a pattern of decorum and a collection of social attitudes which somewhere along the line in the past fifty years have eluded the race of men.

Don't be dismayed by either your problems or the ones the preceding generation has foisted upon you. Don't be upset by the ground rules that you must operate under. And don't surrender even a fraction of your sense of well-being because the planet you occupy is a place of tension and danger. It is also a planet of ferment, of changing ideas, of a sifting and altering of values. These shifts and changes can be for the better. This inheritance of yours is also a challenge to make them precisely that. The potential of this world and its people is unlimited, and this potential is yours also. Have a ball.

ANDRÉ KOSTELANETZ

The Adventure of Discovering

André Kostelanetz, conductor and patron of the arts, has recorded some eighty albums for Columbia alone, which have sold in the neighborhood of fifty million copies. It is estimated that if all the albums of his music were placed in a single pile, they would rise four times as high as Mount Everest. He regularly conducts the New York Philharmonic's spring Promenade Concerts at Lincoln Center which he inaugurated in 1963.

There have always been times in history when man was especially adventuresome and opened new vistas. It strikes me, however, that today we are living in an era when the excitement of discovery is greater than ever. Our adventure has taken us up into space, down under the sea and in all directions over the earth.

We read about outer space and see photographs of our globe taken from thousands of miles above. No longer is life below sea level a secret to us, and through books and pictures we can learn of its mysterious beauties. The airplane has made it possible to visit almost every inhabited place on earth, observe the customs of its people and thrill at its art treasures. Such journeys are no longer a matter of months but only of hours, and the adventure of discovery is at the disposal of millions instead of a few.

Isolation is a concept of the past and most of us have become explorers, if not in action, at least in observation. What an exciting world we live in and what a responsibility we bear not to misuse the privileges now at our disposal!

The excitement of discovery pertains also to the arts. Music has changed people's lives, and a vast majority is truly interested in it. Never before have we had the opportunity to see so many art treasures in so many museums or to see the plays of Euripides, Shakespeare and Molière performed in so many different media. And when it comes to music, I say that more people have discovered it in the past twenty-five years than since the beginning of time. Music has become a part of our daily life not only through increased opportunities to hear it performed in concert halls and opera houses, but through records, radio and, to a smaller degree, television.

I step into a taxi and the driver asks me, "How did the concert sound?" Or there was the little lady who walked into Philharmonic Hall in New York's new Lincoln Center, looked up at Richard Lippold's floating sculpture in the main promenade and asked, "Are these the acoustics?" Young people come up to tell me that they cannot work out school problems without music playing—not just mood music, but Stravinsky's *Firebird* or a Brandenburg Concerto by Bach. Unfortunately, not all music listening is a real adventure. I remember a hotel in Houston. I rode in an elevator run by an elderly woman, and I asked her how she could bear listening to the canned music that played throughout her eight-hour day. She looked at me in surprise. "I never hear it," she said. Or the friend who played with great pride a symphony on his newest stereo equipment. When I asked him how he liked the work, he answered: "Never mind the music. I only played this record to show you how I can stress the highs and lows with this machine." There is also the trend toward background music—music for cooking, music for walking, music for doing nothing and so on. This could create considerable confusion because people who intended to cook might listen to music for doing nothing and wind up going to a restaurant.

And yet the excitement of discovering music in the true sense of the word is overwhelming today. We need only attend a concert which is not part of a regular, sold-out subscription series—a concert to which anyone can buy a ticket. I conduct many such concerts all over the world. Audiences come because they have heard the music on records or radio and now want to enjoy it in a live performance in the company of others. Backstage at Philharmonic or Carnegie Hall they will tell me that I took Ravel's *Daphnis et Chloë* slower or faster than it is played on their record, and then they will add, "You know, we didn't know where Philharmonic Hall was, but it's really not so difficult at all to reach this place." If they ventured forth and crossed the threshold of the concert hall for the first time, what of the audiences in Tokyo who come backstage commenting on the music notes in their programs! They prepare themselves thoroughly at home and read up on the music they are about to hear at a concert and often know points of interest which the program notes do not mention.

Audiences the world over are interested not only in discovering music that is new to them but also in listening to it under different circumstances, and one of these days those responsible for television programming will recognize this fact. Then the finest orchestras, opera companies and soloists will be presented regularly on television, as they are on records and radio.

The ultimate in music listening is not merely the discovery of a new composition or a new way of hearing it, but to experience through repeated exposure to the same work a strong association of ideas and emotions. It is the same in other aspects of life. We return to a certain vacation spot because we have enjoyed ourselves there before; we reread books or plays because we are sure to find new food for thought in them; time and time again we return to the same galleries because we wish to discover new meanings in the same old masterpieces.

The best examples of how man reacts to a piece of music through association of ideas and emotions are the national anthems. If you take the *Marseillaise,* the great French national anthem, and you play it in France for a Frenchman, he is virtually willing to lay down his life and die for France. However, if you were to play this same melody for a Peruvian or for an Eskimo, the chances are that he would find it a rather uninspiring experience.

During World War II, I organized and conducted GI orchestras in different parts of the world. At one particular time we were in Teheran, which was part of the important lend-lease road to the Persian Gulf. At our concert there were to be officials of many allied nations, including Russians, especially Russian generals with huge epaulets. Our commanding general had told me that the Russians had a new national anthem. Moscow had apparently decided that the *Internationale* no longer served its proper function and a new anthem had been composed. The music was ordered from Russia and we barely had time to rehearse it. When we started to play it at the concert, all the generals remained glued to their seats. There was no reaction. Eventually, I noticed a certain elbow movement between them and they began to rise hesitantly to their feet. They didn't know the piece and it meant nothing to them. The association of ideas simply was not there.

In our day, when so many new roads of discovery are open to us all, the greatest sin toward life is—to my way of thinking—not to listen, not to see, not to feel, not to experience—not to live.

MITCH MILLER

The Popularity Explosion

Mitch Miller and his saga began in Roches-ter, New York, where he was born and attended public school and became a base-ball enthusiast. When he decided to learn an instrument for the school band to forestall piano lessons, an oboe was the only one available. As time went by, he became a classical musician (and grew a beard), and then found himself caught up in the postwar pop music explosion. His many Sing Along *albums and TV shows have made his beard a familiar household sight.*

They've added a new virtue for teen-agers to aspire to since I put in my time as one. Of course, we weren't called teen-agers, but we did get advice —all we needed and more—on thrift, honesty, industry and the rest of the catalogue of standard virtues. I'm sure all of this is still being dished up, but today's youngsters are fed even more generously on a subject we rarely heard about—popularity. If the reading matter directed at teen-agers carries any weight, if what absorbs much of the worry time of their parents is significant, the big push is toward popularity—how to achieve it, keep it, expand it and improve it, with your own sex and the other.

This popularity explosion has been with us for some

years, and its value is rarely questioned. I vividly recall that I was forced to appraise it not too long ago in a talk with my younger daughter. (Her sister has made it through to the other side.)

My daughter Margy changed schools when the crush of my busy TV and recording schedule made it necessary to move the family headquarters from the country to a Manhattan apartment. I suppose that for a girl in her mid-teens, entering a new school is easier than spending a season in New Guinea, but I wonder how much. Anyway, Margy made a few friends and got along quite comfortably. As the school year drew to a close, one fellow-student after another approached her with the same message: how very fond of her they all were now, and how much they would have liked to be her friend had they known her earlier. Why, they wanted to know, hadn't Margy let them know sooner what she was *really* like?

And why, Margy asked me with some concern, *hadn't* she made all those friends earlier in the year? Why had it taken them so long to get to know her and like her?

My answer was that I would have been a lot more bothered had she been an instant smash hit in this new setting. To me, that would have indicated that she had made compromises with her true self—with the Margy those of us who really know her love—in order to become popular. Nobody can please everybody, and those who try achieve the sort of lasting values you get blowing a bubble pipe. The people with whom you ought to be friends discover you in good time, and you discover them. The teen-agers who try to force friendships into bloom by opening their innermost thoughts to casual acquaintances are the least likely to make lasting friendships. What's the hurry, anyway? If you have five really close friends in your life-time, you will be doing inordinately well. So, however this relentless pursuit of popularity got started among the young, the one thing to remember about it is that it's unimportant. More than that—it can do you a disservice.

In the years of your life when you should be finding out who you are and what you stand for, the desire to be popular can make you fall in line to look and behave like all the other kids—to lose yourself in a sea of identical hair styles or thought styles.

And still, on all sides I hear parents speak of the rebellion of their teen-age children. I wish it were so, because at that age the kids ought to be separating themselves somewhat from their parents. But rebellion implies a move toward independence, and when you look at this rebellion it turns out to be a revolt en masse—the kids are expressing their differences with their parents as a unit. Instead of striking out boldly on their own, most of them are clutching one another's hands damply for reassurance.

They claim they want to dress as they please, but they all wear the same clothes; they set off in new directions in music, but somehow they end up huddled around the same phonograph record; their reason for thinking or behaving in thus-and-such a manner is that the crowd is doing it. They emerge from their cocoon—into a larger cocoon.

I realize that it has become increasingly tough for a youngster to stand up against the popularity wave and to go his or her own nonconforming way. The pattern of suburban living makes the nonconforming teen-ager stand out like the missionary at the cannibal picnic. And now that industry has firmly carved out a teen-age market, every teen-ager can learn from the ads and the stores what a teen-ager should have. Add to this the fact that many of today's parents have come to award high marks for the popularity of their children, and you have a formidable barrier for the youngster who wants to find his or her own path.

But the barrier is worth scaling, the path is worth pursuing. If you want to listen to Vivaldi instead of going to a slumber party, if you want to collect rocks when everyone is collecting rock and roll, if you want to think some thoughts that you don't care to share at once with your classmates, go to it. Find yourself, be yourself, and popularity will come—with the people who respect you for who you are. That's the only kind of popularity that really counts.

WILLIAM SAROYAN

What's Going On Around Here?

William Saroyan is among the most prolific of American authors. He was twenty-six when he published his first book, a collection of short stories called The Daring Young Man on the Flying Trapeze. *More than twenty have been published since; perhaps the best known is* The Human Comedy. *His most recent novel is* Boys and Girls Together. *He is also a prize-winning playwright. He was born in California and is the father of two children.*

When I was nineteen, I believed on the one hand that I had all the answers, and on the other that having all the answers wasn't enough.

It really didn't mean anything.

This was an attitude of youth, a little on the arrogant side, but all the same slightly appropriate at that stage of the game. If in fact I did *have* all the answers, I knew I didn't have the questions. I wanted people to ask me something, so I could tell them the answer, but nobody seemed to know that I knew everything, and so only rarely did somebody ask me something. Whatever the question, the answer was always easy.

"How do I get to the post office?"

"Two blocks straight ahead."

"Who do you think you are?"

"William Saroyan."

"Hot enough for you?"

"Yes."

Nobody was stunned by the brilliance of these replies, and I waited for the arrival of somebody with a real question.

Before I knew it I was twenty, then thirty, then thirty-five, and there all of a sudden was my son, just born. But he wasn't very good at English, and although I knew he was asking interesting questions all the time, I didn't know what the questions were, although I got the impression that they always translated themselves into one rather large question, "What's going on around here?"

As soon as I knew he had good hearing, I began to tell my son the answer to that question, and I have been doing it ever since. He is now almost nineteen and whenever we meet he asks and I answer, but at the same time I ask and he answers. We talk about everything. I ask him to speak into my left ear because my right ear is kind of reserved for loud music and shouting. It just isn't able to pick up polite speech, and whenever my son and I are being polite I want to hear every word he says.

"The thing that's going on around here," I began to tell him nineteen years ago, "is what we call in the trade *life*. That means, to begin with, that somebody is somebody—as you are somebody. And then it means that all around him is all this classified and unclassified stuff, which is called *world*. It's a funny word, in a way, obviously a garbling of an unfunny word, which is called, of course, *word*, which in turn is said to have been, to be, the thing that *was* in the beginning, perhaps the only thing. Everything was probably always there, but until the word arrived there didn't seem to be very much difference between all, for instance, and nothing. But for a long time there has been a difference on account of the word. All is all, and nothing is nothing, and in between is everything leftover. This leftover stuff is stuff like what we loosely call culture, art, philosophy, religion, anthropology and so on, but you can't eat this stuff. Eat your boiled egg before it gets cold."

"No," my son said in English or in Infancy. "I don't want to eat a boiled egg, I want to eat the moon."

"Well, the fact is the moon *isn't* cheese, and you can't eat the moon, so eat your boiled egg."

"No, I want to eat New York."

"It's too big. There's not enough salt to put on it."

In this manner we had a lot of pleasant talks, and then all of a sudden he got the hang of English and he began to ask questions in that astonishing language.

"What is fire? We make this fire in the fireplace every night, and we watch the fire, but what *is* fire?"

Or at the zoo, about a kangaroo: "Who is *he?*"

Or walking into my study while I am writing a new play, concentrating, thinking about nothing else but the problem of making the play mean something: "Why are you mad?" (He means angry, of course, but even with the inaccurate word, the word with the unintended meaning, the question is valid, because any man who is trying to make a new work of art is in fact mad.)

And then a couple of years later along came his sister and of course I began to answer her questions too. Then she became a teen-ager, because *that's* what's going on around here. Time. The minute somebody starts, personal time starts for him. If somebody *doesn't* start, neither personal time nor any other kind of time starts for him. That makes being somebody and having personal time a kind of big exciting thing. A fellow might not have made it, and then who would ask the questions?

So my daughter says, "If I eat my boiled egg, will I be beautiful, like my mother?"

"Yes."

"I don't want to eat it, because I want to be ugly, like my father, ha ha ha."

Well, now, that isn't bad for a two-year-old native of the city of San Francisco, and so there's loud laughter in the house. Laughter's going on, too, as of course it always has gone on, in a whole great big language all its own— English, Latin, Sanskrit, Greek and so on. Kids make a lot of comedy and laughter as they move along in the simple but also complicated and mysterious business of being themselves, of having their own personal time, of changing, and of changing again.

Aged five, my daughter says, "Will you buy me that cat?"

"That cat's an ocelot."

"What's an ocelot?"

"An ocelot's a kind of wild cat. It really shouldn't be in a cage in a pet store at all."

"Where should it be?"

"Where all the other ocelots are, in the hills and mountains, where the trees are, where ocelots are free. That ocelot is not very happy in that cage."

"Will you buy the ocelot and take him up into the hills and set him free, then?"

"Do you want him to be free?"

"Yes."

"Why?"

"Why should he be in a little cage? We're not in a little cage. Will you buy him and set him free?"

"Yes, if he doesn't cost too much."

Well, the lady in the pet store wants seventy-five dollars for him, and I haven't even got seventy-five dollars for new shoes for everybody, let alone for a captured unhappy ocelot, and so my daughter and I leave the pet shop and she begins to think about things like that. Something being free and then being caught and kept prisoner and sold to somebody for some reason. First, she thinks about ocelots and animals in general, and then all of a sudden she thinks about people.

"Do they catch people and sell them?"

"They used to, but not any more."

"They can't catch me and sell me, can they?"

"No, they can't. But you have to be careful all the time   *158* just the same because it is always possible for anybody to be caught and to be sold, not the way ocelots are, but another way."

"Will you buy me an ice-cream cone, then?"

"Yes."

Thus, talking all the time, every day, hearing a question, answering a question, and then little by little asking these two new people, my son and my daughter, a lot of questions, and hearing their answers, communication goes on, sometimes excellent communication, sometimes not quite successful, and now and then entirely unsatisfactory. And that's when the shouting starts, which also has its importance and fun, especially a week or two later, or a year or two later, or even ten or twenty years later. Because we never really stop trying to figure out, by questions and answers, what is *actually* going on around here. And what we really want to do is find out how to make this whole business mean something somebody can smile about, even though nothing ever stops being rough and tough.

ROSEMARY PARK

Accounting for Taste

Rosemary Park is the only woman ever to head two colleges. Now president of Barnard College in New York City, Miss Park was previously president of Connecticut College for Women for fifteen years. She herself is a Radcliffe graduate and took her Ph.D at the University of Cologne.

As an educator, she believes that the study of history, science and the arts "gives one the confidence to create a style for one's life, to which others may also voluntarily adhere."

"There is no accounting for taste" is an old phrase which we all use to stop discussions. The arguments will usually have centered on whether it is all right to like certain things, certain people, certain kinds of behavior. To most of us the remark means that there is no such thing as good taste, there are only different kinds of taste, and therefore, argument about the whole matter is a fruitless kind of exercise. Another interpretation of the saying, however, could be that it is difficult to account for good taste. This is the meaning I would like to discuss because I agree with it, and because I do not believe that to think about the whole matter of taste is a useless procedure. It may be difficult but it is not unimportant or impossible.

161   It is particularly important for Americans to think about good taste because we are the most influential country in the world today. Our products go into every part of the globe, our movies carry a mirror of our behavior into the most distant villages and our magazines travel too by jet planes and slow-moving cargo ships to all ports of call. We have a grave responsibility not to portray ourselves as vulgar, cheap and ostentatious, three words which are negative predicates of taste, for we will assuredly be imitated everywhere. What goes to make good taste today in America and what can we do to foster it, not only for our own enjoyment but for the picture it gives of us abroad? A few examples will help to show how complicated a subject taste is.

Some years ago, when I was an adviser in a girl's college dormitory, a group of students came to protest a college ruling that no student should come into the dining room for breakfast in pajamas or pin curls. "What is wrong with this? We do it at home, why not here?" said they. Now obviously such behavior is in no sense equivalent to lying, stealing or cheating—actions we would all agree are wrong. However unpleasant breakfasting with hundreds of unwashed, unkempt students may be, no one could really say it is morally wrong. It is unsightly, it is depressing as a way to begin the day; it is, quite simply, in bad taste. The students, however, who used the word "wrong" about this behavior, had unconsciously touched on one of the important elements in good taste. Like morality, good taste recognizes the existence of other people. Good taste requires that we care about other people's feelings sufficiently to discipline our behavior. The schoolchildren who noisily flood into a public bus and trample the other passengers are full, we say, of natural animal spirits. Actually they are unsure enough of themselves so that if one of them begins to scream, they all do, and what the other passengers may think, they don't care. It is rude, vulgar behavior, not wrong but in bad taste. The place for letting go is not in the bus but on the playground, and in a way they all know this but are not strong enough to control themselves. I therefore draw the conclusion that taste has to do with discipline, the power of self-control for the sake of appearance, for the sake of other people.

Self-control is not weakness; it is not lack of exuberance or strength. On the contrary, behavior which is in good taste always hints, I think, at power. It prefers understatement. Perhaps it takes a while until we all discover how much more powerful understatement is. Recently a European friend of mine and I passed a pretty young American girl on the street. She was dressed in skin-tight pants and sweater and my friend, glancing at her, said under his breath, "Poor thing, how obvious!" To emphasize what every female possesses is not really enough to be attractive. She could have been beautiful, but instead she succeeded only in being obvious.

Good taste in dress is hard to achieve. It begins, I think, with understatement. Some of the best-dressed women are college girls whose natural elegance of movement, shining hair and wise selection of color make them, I think, among the most beautiful women in the world. I see generation after generation of them enter college uncertain in behavior, often as obvious in dress as the girl I described. When they graduate, these same girls have learned the art of understatement. They have achieved enough assurance to be themselves and not rely on mere femaleness to be attractive. Some women, no doubt, are born with a proclivity for good taste, just as some of us can carry a tune and some can't. But almost all the girls I know have learned in their college years that simply to shout by their dress and behavior, "Hi, I am female!" is too obvious and simple. Understatement is more attractive in any long-term relationship than strident emphasis on femaleness.

I cannot prove it but I think that besides self-control and understatement there is a genuine intellectual element in some aspects of good taste. That is why the senior in college is so much better dressed than the freshman. But the capacity to dress well is related to other forms of good taste. Since I became a college official, I have seen a very great improvement in interior decorating in college buildings and in college food. This has come about not just because college administrators care but because students care too. It seems a long time ago when a salad in America consisted solely of a piece of lettuce, a slice of tomato and a daub of mayonnaise. And the pictures which students care to hang in their rooms, the records they collect, have little resemblance to the pitiful things I saw as an undergraduate. Good music is more accessible to us all today and college students have taken advantage of this. So, too, the great expansion of our American museums has had its effect on American taste. I hardly ever go into one of our great city art collections without meeting students.

If I were trying to discover what good taste is, I think I would begin by visiting the art museum in my city. At first it may seem boring. This, however, is because most of us have to learn how to look at a picture. To begin with we must realize that if we find the museum boring, the fault lies with us, not with the museum. We are simply too ignorant to appreciate what it offers, and in all humility we need to return again and again and honestly seek out the reason why this is a great portrait, and the magazine cover not, in spite of its cuteness. But why put ourselves through this learning process? Whether we like or dislike a picture or don't know whether we like it does not seem an essential kind of knowledge for living.

The answer to the question depends on how much we want to get out of living. Psychologists tell us that only a small part of the brain has reached its maximum use or development in the human species. The same is probably true of our feelings and taste. If we wish to exploit our possibilities beyond the great mass of human beings who go through life only half using their brains and feelings or sensibilities, then we should care about enlarging our capacities for genuine lasting pleasure. We all possess these capacities for enjoyment, but many of us stop far short of really experiencing the world around us because we never know the educative experience of acquiring good taste. As I have indicated, the first stage is learning to know what other generations have admired—in books, in pictures, in music, in behavior. This is the intellectual element in taste. One has to know that Rembrandt and Beethoven exist before one can learn to appreciate these masters. Then there is a moral element in taste: self-control in appearance for the sake of others. Washing and dressing in the morning may require self-discipline but it makes a pleasanter start for the day's work for all who have to join you at the breakfast table. It shows good taste.

Taste, however, is not an unchanging standard. It varies with the epochs of history, with age and with experience. But I believe these permutations always exist within a certain moral and intellectual framework without being entirely ethical or entirely intellectual in origin and practice. What actually happens in the exercise of taste is a refinement of feeling and of sensitivity. The skin-tight sweater seems too obvious; we come to call it vulgar. The magazine picture of the pink and white baby can be looked at only once and then can say no more to us, while in great paintings of the same subject the child is a source of mystery and never-ending attraction. The pink and white is too easy; we know that life is not like that and we resent the artist's saying so little; we call it cheap. This refinement which comes from our knowledge that one can say more, smell or taste more subtle differences, win by understatement, enhances our personal pleasure in life. The particular artists or colors or textures we love will change but they will always demand more and more sensitivity of us. Cultivation of taste is a lifelong activity, partly conscious, partly unconscious. New experiences are always opening before us. These new horizons of feeling develop, I believe, a greater sense of personal power. Taste, then, is not indulgence but selection and challenge. Just as the lawyers say that the law imposes wise restraints to make men free, so good taste imposes discipline in order that we may experience more widely and deeply the beauty of life and of the human relationships about us.

EUGENE ORMANDY

You Are the Future

Eugene Ormandy, born in Budapest in 1899, is just one year older than the Philadelphia Orchestra, which he has led through some four thousand concerts in the past thirty-two years, as well as in the making of more than two hundred superb albums for Columbia Records. The maestro, a violin prodigy, began his musical career in Hungary at the age of five. He was a professor at the Royal Academy at seventeen. Before coming to the United States, he went on concert tours and taught at the State Conservatory.

Know your land!—its contours, its history, its flavors and its potentials. By so doing you will be better able to shape its destiny. Too often it needs the suggestion from someone foreign to your shores to bring this fact into sharp focus.

Many years ago I asked a native Philadelphian to take me to Independence Hall and to Franklin's grave. To my astonishment he told me that he had never visited them and wasn't even quite sure that he knew where they were located.

In the course of my musical career I have traveled all over the United States, not only conducting the Philadelphia Orchestra on tour, but also guest-conducting the many great orchestras of other cities. I have found myself in Florida and Kansas, Oregon and Arizona, Maine and California. Everywhere I have satisfied my own deep curiosity about their regional characteristics and their histories.

My trips to the West (no longer "wild," alas) have heightened my knowledge of the folk heroes of the past, and while conducting Aaron Copland's ballet suite from *Billy the Kid,* I have felt that much more akin to the music. Similarly, the grandeur of the Grand Canyon is not only a soul-satisfying experience in itself, but it also lends an additional depth to my approach to Ferde Grofé's popular *Grand Canyon Suite,* which is dedicated to that natural wonderland.

The richness of natural beauty and folklore and the differing qualities of the American people—these are limitless, and every American must savor this richness and variety in order to represent best to others what we are. This very "infinite variety" constitutes the unique flavor of our land—perhaps it is its most cherishable aspect.

When an ancient philosopher suggested "Know thyself," he meant more than that you should know yourself as an individual. He also meant that you should know yourself as the focus of many influences and traits, personal and national. As the mouth of a great river contains within its waters the varied contributions of all its upriver tributaries, so you possess within you all the contributions of your forebears—and just as all of this rich accumulation becomes a part of the greater bounty of the sea, so this is your own accumulated richness upon which you will draw for sustenance in the future.

The future of serious music in the United States rests with *you,* both as performers and as listeners. Everything that is accomplished today means *nothing* to the past, means *something* to the fleeting present and means *everything* to the future. And you are the future!

Whenever I conduct a concert I realize that what is achieved during the performance will have a certain permanence in a few minds. But when I have completed a recording session I think of the many, many minds which will hear and rehear such recordings and which will use them as touchstones for future performances. Perhaps it is for this reason that I am sometimes dissatisfied with my recordings. Perfection is, happily, the only goal which constantly beckons, but which can never be achieved.

In the course of almost forty years of music making in the United States, I have been fortunate in coming in contact with young musicians on many occasions, either through competitive auditions or by hearing young groups perform in ensemble. On such occasions I have always been amazed at the vigor of their playing as well as at their splendid technical proficiency.

Recently I heard a performance by the young musicians of the Eastman Philharmonia, which spent three triumphant months touring in Europe, the Soviet Union and the Near East. They played a long and difficult program which would have challenged any of the best professional orchestras in the whole world, and the performance came off with flying colors. The spontaneity and freshness of their musical outlook pulsed through every bar, and I knew then that our musical future was assured.

Too, as I listened, I thought of the nature of the sacrifice that these young people are making. They devote all of their youthful years to conquering the demands of their instruments and to becoming acquainted with an already vast and ever-growing musical literature. Their individual futures (with very few exceptions) are ones of complete anonymity in the ranks of large symphonic groups. Yet because of their love for music, they willingly make these sacrifices—not just for themselves but for you and for all future audiences who constitute the beneficiaries of their years of sacrifice.

Now I don't imply that such selfless behavior is anything new—music students have done this for centuries all over the western world. But *this* is the important thing: Never have young people been tempted from that life of sacrifice by such exciting and profitable futures as lie waiting for the young people of America. I have read of the desire for "middle-of-the-road security" by many students. But personally, I have never believed that this is true, because the challenges of the future are too great. That a young American can resist the beguilements of the Space Age to devote himself to the musical values of the past and to a lifetime of stirring the audiences of the future—this proves to me that the mere comfort of mediocrity is *not* your generation's goal.

When I arrived in the United States forty years ago, I came to what was known as "the land of opportunity." (You know, I always like to explain that I was born in the United States at the age of twenty-two.) Well, America *was* the land of opportunity, and, thank God, is *still* such an exciting land! The whole world knows of its automobiles, its gadgetry and of its fantastic "know-how," but does this same world know of its even greater cultural future? I think that the answer is: *Yes, but they don't know enough.* Think of the impact that the Eastman ensemble must have had upon the audiences in Moscow, Cairo and Athens—young American instrumentalists performing music by great American composers! This is one of the challenges which is faced by our country—a challenge which only the younger generation can meet: carrying the exciting story of America to the people of other lands.

When the Philadelphia Orchestra toured Western Europe and some of the countries behind the Iron Curtain several years ago, I was proud of the fact that the orchestra numbered almost ninety percent native-born Americans in its ranks. That proud claim could not have been made a generation ago. President Eisenhower knew the immense value of this fact when he established his famous "People-to-People Program" some years ago, and

President Kennedy wisely increased the activity of our cultural groups in reaching across the seas.

Too long have we looked abroad for stimulus and direction. Now we have arrived at a time when such seeking is mutual and increasingly fruitful. How fortunate you are to be in the enviable position to reap the harvest of so provocative an international exchange!

ROBERTA PETERS

The Seven-year Cinderella

Roberta Peters has been one of the New York Metropolitan Opera Company's leading coloratura sopranos since her debut fourteen years ago. Among her many recordings are Mozart's Magic Flute *for DGG.* The Music of Leonard Bernstein *for Command and, for RCA Victor, Mozart's* Marriage of Figaro, *Rossini's* Barber of Seville, *Gluck's* Orfeo ed Euridice, *and Richard Strauss'* Ariadne auf Naxos. *When not performing here or abroad, she settles down as the wife of a hotel-chain owner and mother of two boys.*

Whenever people talk about "overnight" success or "Cinderella stories," there's something they often seem to forget—all the years of struggle, heartache and disappointment that came before. Even Cinderella herself scrubbed many a floor and swept many a cinder before her Fairy Godmother came along.

When I made my Metropolitan Opera debut at the age of twenty, it seemed to reviewers then (and even now!) a true-to-life Cinderella tale, a Hollywood-type "overnight" success story. The newspapers made a lot of the "unknown young singer who was called to replace the ailing star of that evening's performance before a sold-out house." At that time, I was already under contract to the Metropolitan Opera but was not scheduled to make my debut until a few months later. It was, of course, a wonderful opportunity, but what everyone tended to gloss over was that for seven years, from the time I was thirteen, my every effort and my whole life had been completely devoted to studying opera. The "overnight" success had been, in reality, a long and difficult journey. And when the moment came, I was ready.

In retrospect, I look back on those years with bittersweet memories, for I regret, even today, all the things I missed when I was a teen-ager. In order to concentrate completely on my musical studies, I left school for private tutoring. I studied piano, voice, French, German, Italian, drama, deportment, ballet—everything that was necessary for a musical career. For I knew this was what I wanted and realized it would be a long, hard battle and would demand financial sacrifice on the part of my parents. Because of this, I never had the fun of high school days, the dates, the parties and that wonderful feeling of just being young. I never truly had the companionship of people my own age because my private studies thrust me into an adult world. I had cast my lot, and there could be no compromise. Even now, I still regret the fact that I never went to a prom.

They were pretty lean and lonely years, and there were setbacks and discouragements. I can remember many days when, after a disappointing lesson, I would wander alone by the Ninety-sixth Street Reservoir in New York City and wonder whether the struggle was really worth it. Maybe those well-meaning friends and relatives were right—maybe I *had* set my goal too high.

Then, when I was sixteen, I had what seemed a wonderful offer—a chance to star on Broadway in Kurt Weill's *Street Scene*. It seemed like a golden opportunity, and it would have meant an end to my family's financial struggle, for both my mother and father were working to pay for the high cost of my private studies. But every road has its detours, and I realized this was one. The strain of singing nightly in a Broadway show can wreak havoc with a coloratura voice. But more important, this was not my goal—I wanted the world of opera, not the bright lights of Broadway. So with some regret, I turned down that offer, and in doing so learned the marvelous quality of patience. Many times I wondered if I had done the right thing. But then, four years later, my chance finally came.

History is full of stories about people in every walk of life who seem to have suddenly catapulted into the spotlight of their chosen field, whether it be music, art, literature, science, politics—even religion! And so often, the term "overnight" success is applied to them. I always feel there is a certain quality that distinguishes these people from those who "had a lucky break." This quality, I think, is having the courage of your own convictions. And this courage generally necessitates "going it alone."

It is not easy to devote yourself completely to your chosen goal, and it takes a lot of guts, tenacity and inner strength to go it alone. In this age of conformity, with big corporations and stereotyped suburbia, it is difficult to remain an individual, with ideas of your own. The world is always full of people who think you're crazy for even trying and of those who are certain you will never make it.

Being an individual and doing what *you* want are particularly difficult during the teen-age years, when the approval of your crowd means so much. That's when the courage of your convictions gets its first test: Everyone's going to the big game, but you really should study for your math exam or write the essay for the literary contest or baby-sit if every penny counts for your college education. It's only human nature to want to be liked and to go along with the dictates of your crowd. It's always a lot easier to join them, to do what they do, to think their way. But if there is something you want and have to do, there comes a time when you must go it alone.

Right now, there are probably people you know who are devoting themselves to something they want and
175 believe in. Chances are they're not winning any popular-

ity contests. Their clothing and hairdos aren't up to the minute, they don't get around so much and maybe don't even date often. But honestly, don't you envy them? And don't you respect them for their courage to be individuals?

It was the courage of convictions, this individual spirit, that gave birth to our country, pushed its frontiers westward and built it into the greatest nation the world has ever known. And the people who did these things were "loners" who knew that the saddest thing is not to have failed, but never to have made the attempt.

For many years, few recognized the genius of Albert Einstein. How many serums did Dr. Salk discard before the polio vaccine was perfected? How many people advised the famous Metropolitan Opera tenor Jan Peerce that he was fine for Radio City Music Hall, but he could never sing at the Met? The Hollywood stars who "suddenly" became sensations usually pounded the pavements and ate peanut-butter sandwiches for many years.

Success in what you want is not easy to achieve, and there's no guarantee you'll ever make it. It may take quite some time for it to visit you, and it can be a lonely and discouraging wait. But when it happens, there's always someone who'll say to you: *"How does it feel to be an overnight success?"*

I'll wager some people at the ball asked Cinderella that question.

MAX SHULMAN

Humor Is No Laughing Matter

Max Shulman was lucky. A publisher caught his undergraduate work in the University of Minnesota newspaper and urged him to "fire off" his first novel, Barefoot Boy with Cheek. *Now, seven novels (including* Rally Round the Flag, Boys! *and his newest,* Anyone Got a Match?), *two plays and hundreds of stories later, Mr. Shulman lives in Connecticut and is the father of four children.*

The humor market is booming. Television, the movies, Broadway, book and magazine publishers—all are hollering for more comedy. Small wonder, then, that so many young people with literary talent who have heretofore confined themselves to serious writing are beginning to cast an appraising eye at comedy.

Well, young people with literary talent who have heretofore confined yourselves to serious writing, listen to this old veteran, battle-scarred and weary. If you're thinking of switching to comedy writing, here is some advice: forget it.

You'll never learn comedy. I don't care how talented you are; you'll never learn it. It *can't* be learned. Either you have it or you don't.

And what is this mysterious "it" you either have or do not? It's not a technique, not a formula, not a procedure, not a set of rules. It is an *eye*—an askew eye, an awry eye, an antic eye, a cockeye. It's an eye that sees the world in that oblique and unexpected way we call comedy.

Where does one get such an eye? How, in other words, do you get to be a humorist? The hard way, friends, the hard way.

Dr. Freud and his followers have written big, fat learned books about the sources of humor. What it boils down to is this: Humor is a defense of the disadvantaged. If you are born poor or ugly or unloved or a member of an oppressed minority or emotionally unstrung or spiritually unglued and you find you can't face the world as it is, you develop an eye that reshapes the world so that it becomes tolerable to look upon.

I don't suggest, mind you, that all the earth's unfortunates become humorists. Most become the opposite; they turn to such neurotic pursuits as crime, drugs and the advertising business. No, I don't say all neurotics are humorists, but I do say—and I'll say it with my last breath—that all humorists are neurotics. When you get a chance, read some biographies of famous humorists. It makes *The Lower Depths* seem like a month in the country. Such towering despair! Such abysmal gloom! And yet, as neurotics go, I think you'll find them a pretty fetching bunch. For all their traumas, they still didn't curl up in the fetal position and quit. Bravely they stood on their spindly legs and fired off their salvos of paper bullets.

So, young people with literary talent who have heretofore confined yourselves to serious writing, I urge you to stick with your serious writing. Stay away from humor unless you are prepared to be born again and to go through a traumatic childhood. Remember, a humorist is a humorist *before* he is a writer. It's not a thing you can learn, no matter how hard you study, how long you practice. You've got it early or not at all.

And what if you are one who's got it? What if you see

funny and think funny and write funny? How do you become a professional comedy writer?

You become a professional comedy writer the way you become any kind of professional writer: You write.

And what do you write about? You write what anybody else writes about.

Do I mean that the subject of a serious story can also be the subject of a humorous story? That is precisely what I mean. Norman Mailer and Thomas Heggen both wrote about the Pacific during World War II. Mailer wrote *The Naked and the Dead* and Heggen wrote *Mister Roberts*. Truman Capote and Mark Twain both wrote about southern children. Capote wrote *Other Voices, Other Rooms* and Twain wrote *Tom Sawyer*. Nathaniel Hawthorne and George Axelrod wrote about adultery. Hawthorne wrote *The Scarlet Letter* and Axelrod wrote *The Seven-Year Itch*.

It's the humorist's eye, not the topic, which determines whether a work is funny. Even death can be hilarious, as witness *Arsenic and Old Lace*. A quick look at the current crop of "sick" jokes will show you how far you can go with humor and, according to some, still be funny.

Let me be perfectly clear here. I don't mean that bad taste, gore, violence and ugliness are intrinsically funny. All I mean is that no aspect of the human condition will be off limits to the humorist.

All right then. If you're a humorist, what are you waiting for? You've got the time, you've got the talent, you've got an audience palpitating for comedy. All you need now is stamina, perseverance and the will to win.

And a little bit of luck won't hurt.

BURL IVES

Dear Wayfarers:

Burl Ives, one of six children, was born in Hunt City Township, Jasper County, Illinois, of a singing family. After sampling college, he left during the depression to roam the country as a vagabond, soaking up folk songs as he went. He washed dishes, sang on the radio, traveled with a tent show and became lead singer for a touring evangelist; eventually he found his way to New York. He has since made a very large mark on the world as a balladeer, actor, writer and personality extraordinary.

As I put pen to paper to each and all of you, my favorite set of Shakespeare is at hand, for

This morning, like the spirit of a youth
That means to be of note, begins betimes

and so did I. You have time on your side: I, experience on mine; so what shall we exchange but my experiences for your time?

These I give you willingly, for I never gave a friend anything I wouldn't want myself, especially not good advice; the latter, on the traditional grounds that "you get no thanks for it." I held my own counsel until the day came when I couldn't resist any further and I bestowed my first recorded good advice upon the music lovers of this land, which to my great surprise reaped me a very tangible form of thanks. The bard, in this case, was Bob Merrill, and the advice:

> As you go through life, make this your goal,
> Watch the doughnut . . . not the hole.*

Mind you, I had been "watching the doughnut" with my mind's eye ever since I began wayfaring down the road at the age of sixteen. As my eyes opened up to the world around me, I found fascinating things to see; as my mind opened too, I became aware of even more. More importantly, I found the unwritten code of the wayfarer, which, if put into words, might run as follows: "Why wait till a man is starved before you share your bread with him?"

My banjo and my dreams of seeing mighty mountains, silver rivers, wide sweeping plains, magnificent cities and a nation of people I knew nothing of took me a long way down the road from Hunt City, Illinois, to New York City, where the friends I made, I am happy to say, have stayed my friends always.

One day I was sitting on a park bench in Central Park in the middle of New York City figuring out my first broadcast for NBC. It was my big chance. Luckily, I had been reading Thomas Wolfe:

> Which of us has known his brother,
> Which of us has looked into his father's heart,
> Which of us has not forever remained prison pent,
> Which of us is not forever a Stranger and alone? †

From Wolfe's words I thought of the melody of a beautiful old song, *I'm Just a Poor Wayfaring Stranger*. And

* *The Doughnut Song*, by Bob Merrill, © copyright 1950 by Anne-Rachel Music Corporation, New York, N.Y. Used by permission.

† From *Look Homeward, Angel* by Thomas Wolfe. Copyright 1929 by Charles Scribner's Sons. Copyright renewed 1957 by Edward C. Aswell, Administrator, C.T.A., Estate of Thomas Wolfe.

that was what gave me the idea of becoming the Wayfaring Stranger. "I will let my beard grow," I thought, getting up. "The Wayfaring Stranger should have a beard."

And that became the "style" of Burl Ives, the Wayfaring Stranger. By style, I mean the equal ease with which a person can wear ragged jeans or Sunday-best . . . the way you pick up a guitar and sing to say something, whether shaping history or singing up the richness of history inherited.

The Beatles or Joan Baez or you—your style is as uniquely a part of your character as is the mole on your wherever-it-is. Style is taking a bolt of cotton, the blue sea, the musical scale and the colors of the rainbow and making them distinctly your own . . . like the spark of life inside you.

And should the spark ignite the Marco Polo in you to wayfare across the country or around the world, as it does in all of us Americans, may you travel in style . . . *your* style. As for tips on style, here are a few, courtesy of William Shakespeare:

At the bistro: Have more than thou showest,
Speak less than thou knowest,
Lend less than thou owest.
At Passport Control: All orators are dumb, where beauty pleadeth.
Everywhere you go: Let all the ends thou aim'st at be thy country's,
Thy God's, and truth's.

Times haven't changed since I sat in the park. Joan Baez, Bob Dylan and Peter, Paul and Mary still sing of the same things. I find no real difference between myself and young men of today. They have beards. They all have guitars.

When I sat in the park that day, I was at the beginning of a long career. Let me tell you what happened.

The Day Came. I sang my theme and the announcer told a coast-to-coast network that the Wayfaring Stranger was coming down the road with a bagful of songs. At the end of the program, the director came out and said, "A very good beginning. But I have bad news for you." My heart sank. Fired! "Your program was interrupted by a news flash which took up the whole fifteen minutes. France has capitulated. Better luck next week."

The weeks passed and I received favorable comments. One day I was putting my guitar in the case after a broadcast when I was called to the control room for a long-distance call from Sarasota, Florida. "For me?" I knew no one in Florida.

I lifted the receiver and said, "Hello." A wild, enthusiastic voice bellowed, "Hello, are you Burl Ives?" I quickly moved the phone a foot from my ear to protect the eardrum and admitted I was.

The voice said that he had heard my first song and had called his children back, although they had started for school. He said he didn't care if they missed school, songs like this were more important: "These songs are the soil of America. These songs are great poetry. I've never heard anything like it, and I've heard singing all over America." I interrupted to thank him. "Don't thank me," he yelled back. "I thank you." By this time I was yelling too. I screamed, "What's your name?"

"MacKinlay Kantor."

"The writer?"

"Sure."

"I've just finished your book, *The Voice of Bugle Ann*."

"You did!" He yelled to someone with him, "Irene! He just finished *Bugle Ann*." He laughed aloud and shouted, "Burl, I'm gonna be in New York in a few weeks. Where can I get in touch with you? I want you to meet Carl."

"Who's Carl?"

"Sandburg. He'll go crazy over your stuff. Give me your address. I want us to be friends." And so it was to be.

Young people today, more than at any other time, know that an ounce of irreverent humor is worth a ton of false reverence.

Humor is the flowering of the human intelligence into its greatest irrelevancies, by which we get the most meaningful glimpses into our fellow man and ourselves.

It is the best way I know to handle the people you meet along the way, who try to goldbrick you "pat" ideas. For them, I distilled a handful of capsule solutions, of which here are a few:

Girls:

Give a man ground on which to stand
And you'll understand him.

Men:

Give a woman a chance to change her mind;
The two sides of her you'll find.

True-badours:

Travel with seven strings to your guitar:
E, A, D, G, B, E . . . and a shoestring.

True-amours:

A good Mulligan stew is like life itself:
You only get out of it what you put in.

Voters:

Look to the left and look to the right
And you'll never ever get run over.

MARIANNE MOORE

Profit Is a Dead Weight

Marianne Moore is America's most-awarded living poet. She was born in St. Louis, Missouri, in 1887, and went to Bryn Mawr College. After receiving her degree, she taught commercial subjects at the United States Indian School in Carlisle, Pennsylvania, worked in the New York Public Library and edited a poetry magazine called The Dial. *She is a member of the American Academy of Arts and Letters. Among her books,* A Marianne Moore Reader *samples her poems, essays and letters.*

Overinitiative has something to be said for it. With no resistance, a kite staggers and falls; whereas if it catches the right current of air it can rise, darting and soaring as it pulls and fights the wind. Overinitiative can take us somewhere. Humility is yet mightier, can sometimes retrieve a situation; as when the bear cub in Frank Buck's jungle camp escaped through a half-closed cage door, grew tired and hungry, hurried back, tripping over a python which looked like a fallen tree, and reached camp safe, merely because the snake was asleep and moved but an inch or two. An exception doesn't prove the rule. The next python may not have just had a meal or may not be asleep.

187   I call these reflections *Profit Is a Dead Weight*—a sentence I happened on in my Italian dictionary: *Lucro è peso morto*—because, although pride is usually regarded as the worst of the seven deadly sins, greed seems to me the vice of our century. Why should I pay "twenty dollars for the set" when I want *only* a portfolio, *no* paper knife and *no* brass gold pen? If I buy a chance and win a watch that was paid for by neighbors who bought a chance with hard-earned money needed for food, did I profit? The root of the struggle to win something for nothing is covetousness. Do we have to be like the man who killed the hen who laid the golden eggs—overcome by greed to want all of them at once—and found only what he would have found in an ordinary hen? He had cut the magic chain and she would never lay again.

Behavior: it all reduces to a moral issue. We must not want something from another so much that we steal it; cannot kill another and benefit. Of morals bearing on sex, I hear more than I used to; of trial marriage as reasonable and different from delinquency, an evasion of the moral law, I would say: no innovation, it is as old as mankind.

Among assets that one cannot ignore is the power of concentration. A preamble on television or snatch of Victrola music is not part of it. Can you ignore a disparaging comment, insult, slander? Smother desire for revenge? Make allowance for the defiant salesman who writes, goes on writing and will not look up, the traffic man hardened to explanation? The asset of assets was summed up by Confucius when asked, "Is there a single principle that you can practice through life to the end?" He said, "Sympathy. What you don't want, don't inflict on others."

In the last war, as a man who had survived a bayonet charge was thinking he might somehow escape, he heard a groan; then, "Nigger, pull this bayonet out of my chest." Hardened by the term of disdain, he hesitated, then pulled the bayonet out for the victim and "drug him a mile," as the story was told me. The surgeon treating the bayonet wound said, with a nod toward the Negro, "You owe your life to that man." The Negro and rescued man become friends and, after discharge from the army, shared dinners and holidays whenever possible. "And do you believe that faked-up story?" I was asked, the facts being known to me. How discuss verity with cynics—cynicism being a plant with no fruit or interesting seed? As Confucius says, "If there be a knife of resentment in the heart, the mind fails to attain precision." Defamation, denigration, ridicule, are easy compared with the ability to portray magnanimity—defined by a commentator (via Webster) as "loftiness of spirit enabling one to bear trouble calmly, disdain revenge and make sacrifices for worthy ends."

And what are worthy ends? Knowledge made possible by an overpowering desire to possess it; usefulness—like that of Dr. Squibb, whose pure ether and reliable ether mask were "for use by all who needed them," never patented; saving a boy's severed arm, approximating bone and nerve ends, whereas loss would have made the loser a cripple. Small (if small) ingenuities: one would like to have invented the zipper fastener, epoxy glue, the collapsible dustpan, the figure-eight stitch closure of the hide cover of the baseball.

Sound technique is indispensable to the musician, painter, engineer, mechanic, athlete, fencer, boxer. One does not associate compassion, humility or modesty with boxing. Yet here it is—"that talent which is death to hide" and a boy "wrapped up in it," speedball and pendulum, walking in heavy sand to strengthen the leg muscles; with an aptitude for "invention": a boy "coming up from a dungeon of darkness," in danger of being wasted, inhibited by false accusations—portrayed by Floyd Patterson in *Victory over Myself.* "It was a grind," he says, "but a way out for me and my family." The victory involved "application and concentration"—age-old formula for results in any kind of work, profession, art, recreation—"powerful feeling and the talent to use it"!

"It should not be a case of sink or swim," Floyd Patter-

son says. "You have to learn to walk before you can run";
he (the pathos of it) having had to be *taught* to like being
alive—at the Wiltwyck School in Esopus (New York),
largely, he feels, by Miss Vivian Costen: "The only way I
knew to thank her," he says, "was to be what she wanted
me to be"; his repressiveness continuing a long, long time
as "commensurate power" was emerging. Of coming to the
Olympic Games he says, "I had to come four thousand
miles to really begin to feel that I was like everybody
else." Then, "When they handed out our official clothes,
I could hardly believe my eyes. How do you describe the
feelings somebody like myself can have at a time like
that?" Having won the United States middleweight cham-
pionship—never having bowed before—he says, "I placed
one hand on my stomach and the other on my back . . .
and bent low from the waist. . . . I don't know how long
I remained in that pose. Long enough, anyhow, for somebody to say, 'All right now, Floyd.' Then I straightened
up." The "feelings" are described "with perception at the
height of passion"—letting Henry James say it for me. I
doubt that anyone who is incurably interested in writing,
as I am, and always doing it, has had as much difficulty as
I have in expressing what I find myself fanatically determined to say: How get it all in—compact, unmistakable—
set down as if spontaneously? This book by Floyd Patterson with Milton Gross much intensifies my interest in writing—explicit, vivid, modest—every sentence enchaining
the attention: "the dignity of equality" there on the page,
for beginner or expert to examine at leisure.

    After the conferring of contest awards for verse in a
school which I visited, a teacher * chiefly responsible for
the zeal of the participants said in addressing the students:
"You have daring, courage to believe in yourselves, craftly
skill to produce that which is new and worthy of man as
he was meant to be"; a combat warrant for scholastic
effort applicable generally, one hopes.

   * J. L. Fenner.

"Recreation" can be punishment, and I have, like others, sometimes deplored television for misusing its possibilities. Sometimes, however, it has fired my imagination with gratitude, as when I heard Andrés Segovia playing Boccherini, his fingers moving about among the strings of the guitar like hornet legs flickering here and there over a peach to determine its sweetness. I found absorbing also—although by no means similar—Mr. William Longendecker, an amateur of rhinoceros language, demonstrating his ability to mellow one of the animals by resting a hand on its head and imitating its speech.

Talent is a joyous thing—able to substitute the spirit of praise for the garment of heaviness; or so I thought when hearing—on television—Jean Renoir, son of the painter, interviewed at his home. Asked concerning his childhood, "Would you say you were poor?" he said, "It depends on what you mean. My mother could do much with little. We were always surrounded by luxury in all that is done with the hand." *

Talent, knowledge, humility, reverence, magnanimity involve the inconvenience of responsibility or they die. To the bonanza, the legacy, the professional hit, it would be well if our attitude were that of the poor Brazilian seeking diamonds, dazzled by unearthing a *caldeirão* (cluster of diamonds): "My Lord and Heavenly Father, if this endangers my soul, let it vanish." † It is what every poem is about, as Robert Frost writes, "the triumph of the spirit over the materialism by which we are being smothered."

Example is needed, not counsel; but let me submit here these four precepts:

Feed imagination food that invigorates.

Whatever it is, do it with all your might.

---

* Interview with Winston Burdette, July 23, 1961.

† *The Diary of Helena Morley,* translated by Elizabeth Bishop. Farrar, Straus & Cudahy, 1957.

Never do to another what you would not wish done to yourself.

Say to yourself, "I will be responsible."

Put these principles to the test, and you will be inconvenienced by being overtrusted, overbefriended, overconsulted, half adopted, and have no leisure. Face that when you come to it.

BENNETT CERF

Have a Dream

Bennett Cerf is a man of varied occupations: chairman of the board of Random House, TV panelist on What's My Line? *and newspaper columnist* (Try and Stop Me). *He is also a lecturer and a compiler of humor anthologies. He was born in New York in 1898, attended Columbia University, where he edited the humor magazine, and became a newspaper columnist. After spending a few years in Wall Street, he entered the field of book publishing, to the delight of fun-loving bibliophiles.*

I had just finished giving a lecture in a large, top-ranking midwestern university and, at the request of the dean, I lingered to answer questions put to me by members of the freshman class.

They were a gay, alert lot, seventeen years old on the average, and we got along famously until suddenly I asked *them* a question. "What," I demanded, "do you boys and girls expect to do when you graduate from college?"

I was met by a lot of blank looks. Nor did this surprise me. It had happened to me before. In fact, if I have a single criticism to level at the seventeen-year-olds of today—and on the whole I think the breed is so far ahead of the seventeen-year-olds of my generation that comparisons are embarrassing—it is that too many of them enroll in college and complete their whole four-year course without giving one serious thought to what they're going to do when they're faced with the necessity of going out into the world and making a living.

What's the result? Instead of winding up in the kind of job they are really fitted for and will enjoy performing, more often than not they impulsively take the first reasonably attractive offer that comes along, and thereby frequently get stashed away for life in a kind of routine for which they are temperamentally unfitted and which they ultimately come to loathe.

By the time the misfits realize their mistake, it's often too late to do anything about it. They've already incurred too many obligations: wives, babies, unpaid-for homes and automobiles—plus the gnawing fear that it's too late to switch to something that really attracts them. Necessity and inertia have done their dirty work.

By the time I had reached my seventeenth birthday, I knew exactly what I was going to do when I graduated from college. I was going to be a book publisher—and nothing in the world was going to stop me. This determination enabled me to devote every major activity of my university days—both curricular and extracurricular —to preparing myself for the career I had chosen. It dictated the college I picked (The Pulitzer School of Journalism at Columbia), the undergraduate activity for which I enlisted (the campus "funny" magazine, *The Jester,* where I began a study of American humor that has stood me in good stead ever since) and the nonrequired courses in which I enrolled (literature, history and more literature). The day a diploma was placed in my hot little hands, I could honestly go to a publisher and say I had something to offer him in the way of special training.

Citing my own experiences invariably interests a few students, but I can almost hear most of them saying to themselves, "What does that old fraud know about the kind of world that confronts a young man or woman starting out in life today?" Come to think of it, I probably said the same thing way back in 1920 at Columbia when a comparable graybeard appeared to cast a few pearls of wisdom.

The famous Professor Charles Townsend Copeland of Harvard once said, "Speakers have been showering Cambridge undergraduates with bright thoughts for years and years, and if all their valuable advice were laid end to end, it would still be just as good as new. So little of it ever has been used!"

"Decide what I want to be when I'm only seventeen?" some students ask me. "Suppose I change my mind after I've started?" The answer to that, of course, is that no decision of this kind is irrevocable. All that will have been lost in such a pregraduation shift will be a few hours spent in courses no longer essential. Obviously, if a student has no idea at all in which direction he means to travel, he'll waste just as much time or more in irrelevant studies. Worse still, he may discover he has gone to the wrong school entirely, in the wrong part of the country and with the wrong kind of teachers.

My own business, as I have said, is book publishing, so I know what hardships a number of writers who are famous today endured in order to achieve a career they had determined upon in their youth. John Steinbeck, for instance, carried bricks. Jerome Weidman delivered rented tuxedos. William Faulkner wrote his first novel while serving as a clerk in the Oxford, Mississippi, post office.

The head of one graduate writing course, in fact, determined to learn just how dedicated his students were to the profession they had chosen and made them answer this question: "Coleridge was a drug addict. Poe was an alcoholic. Marlowe was killed by a man whom he was treacherously attempting to stab. Pope took money to keep a woman's name out of a satire, then wrote the piece so she could be recognized anyhow. Chatterton killed himself. Gibbon slaved for years over his formidable *Decline and Fall of the Roman Empire*. When he presented the finished manuscript to his patron, England's Duke of Gloucester (brother of King George III), the Duke's only comment was, 'What? More of these damned, fat, square books? Always scribble, scribble, scribble, eh, Mr. Gibbon?' Are you still *sure* you want to be a writer—and if so, why?" Every student in the class answered yes. They knew what they wanted!

I'm convinced that if any seventeen-year-old today would interview the fifty people in American life he envies and respects the most, he would discover that ninety percent of these outstanding personalities are doing the work that they love and that they knew they were going to do from the time they were old enough to make up their minds.

I must tell you that of all the boys I met this year, the one who was absolutely surest of his destiny was a lad who had his heart set on becoming—of all things—a tree surgeon.

Here's hoping he never falls out of one of his patients!

IGOR STRAVINSKY

A Perfect Total

Igor Stravinsky, a composer of genius, has been in the vanguard of serious music for many decades. When his ballet Rite of Spring *was first played in Paris in 1913, riots broke out in the auditorium. He has said that "people are taught to have too much respect for music; they should be taught to love it instead." Stravinsky was born in 1882 in Russia. He began composing at the age of nine, and later studied with Rimsky Korsakov after a spell at law school. An extremely versatile composer, Stravinsky is probably best known for his ballet scores, like* Petrouchka *and* The Firebird. *He has conducted most of his works in definitive recordings for Columbia. Alfred A. Knopf has published* Thenus and Episodes *(including this article), by Stravinsky and Robert Craft, his long-time collaborator.*

QUESTION: What are the general problems of young people who wish careers as composers or artists—not the timeless problems of art, but those peculiar to our age of science?

ANSWER: Generality itself may be the greatest problem. The arts in past cultures interpreted, symbolized or adorned general ideas—call them religious beliefs, or merely "ends." Now the general as well as the particular ideas of science are incomprehensible to most artists and are likely to remain so in the near future. How, then, is an artist who aspires to associations of science to interpret, symbolize and adorn general scientific beliefs which he is able to apprehend only through an intermediate and inexact language of words? In fact, how is he even to make his representations against them in the event that, like myself, he objects to being taken on a ride to an unannounced destination straphanging to concepts he does not understand? I can say that *my* generalities, cosmological, philosophical, theological, are those of a remote and comparatively primitive past; or, alternatively, my art is my generality. But this is no help to young people whose work is yet to be fashioned. Thank heaven (or some other generality) that I only name the problems, not try to solve them!

Another large problem, and one in which I have had some experience, is the increasing domination by technical processes—call them "means." Closely related to this, in fact a chief consequence of it, is the problem of the accelerating turnover of artistic conventions. I should stop at these two, on which I have some views, and try to disentangle myself from the wool of my own generalities, except that there is one more "problem" on my list and it is the only one on which I am really qualified to speak. This is the problem of old age, of continuing to grow from your seventeen to my eighty-three. The new science of gerontology is of no avail here, and old age is more than ever a nightmare, even to the few near-nonagenarian newsworthies like myself who have escaped that neglect which is the fate of the elderly. As I see it, much of the responsibility for this state of affairs lies with the news-drugged public's obsession with novelty, for our society tends to glamorize, rather than merely encourage, the newest and youngest, the first novels and the Opus 1's, and always at the expense of mature work. This is a side effect of the disintegration of those general ideas.

QUESTION: What do I mean by encroaching technical processes and the consequences thereof?

ANSWER: The present development of recording technique is the nearest example to hand, though the technical aspect of recording is only one of the problems created by an industry that will soon be bringing the most "in" composers' latest gimmicks to Djakarta, Stanleyville and Des Moines directly from the launching pads in the European fashion centers; the distribution of printed music has little effect today in comparison to the distribution of recordings, not only because recordings can be broadcast, but also because most new music cannot be heard in the imagination simply by reading the score, as was once the case. Still, the prospect of world standardization dismays me less than the prospect of the complete technical domination of the musical performance itself. Recording processes, which are determined by wasteful competition, have already arrived at the stage where the manufactured performance has supplanted the true one and where, on choice, most of us would reject the true. We are so well accustomed to the refinements of technical processing even now, in fact, that we find the natural to be less and less allowable. Natural balance, natural dynamics, natural echo, natural color, natural (and endearing) human error—such as the cracked horn-notes which disappeared from recorded performances a decade ago but which still occur in concerts—these have been replaced by added echo and reverberation, by a neutralizing dynamic range, by filtered sound, by an engineered balance. The resulting product is a super-glossy chem-fab music-substitute that was never heard on sea or land, including Philadelphia. Now, obviously, gross and distracting errors must be edited out, and some other improvements should be allowed if the vital cohesion of the performance is not thereby intercepted; but sound engineers and tape splicers have exceeded this kind of minor surgery by so much that they are, in effect, reconducting the performances. And it is already too late to complain, for fake phonography has overtaken fake photography, and a recording nowadays has been so thoroughly "corrected" technically that it is as unlike a live performance as a painted corpse in a Hollywood mortuary is unlike a living human being.

QUESTION: What do I mean by the word convention?

ANSWER: Something quite comprehensive, but as my idea of it probably impinges on other concepts, I doubt that I can offer a definition. I could begin by saying that I am a conventional composer myself, for instance, but that would shed no light, as I am unable to imagine any other kind. Or I could turn to some of the labels habitually cast in opposition to "conventional," like "revolutionary" and "spontaneous," but the artists who would profess to these invoked attitudes would soon prove to have their conventions too, however different the emphasis they would put on the word. Let me discard some meanings which are *not* mine. Conventional is often wrongly equated with old-fashioned. Thus automobile tail fins, jazzy glasses, snoods, were fashions of the fifties, but the principle governing their appearance is a convention both of our economic life and of a certain area of our artistic life. The word is also applied to a kind of art which carries over from its immediate legacy with little change. This is a description, by the way, of most commercially successful art (Rachmaninoff, for example). However, these are not my meanings. To me, conventions are codes of agreement. They are carriers of tradition, but differ from traditions in that they are modified rather than developed, and in that they are tied to this or that time, whereas traditions, as major lines of descent, are timeless. Traditions may be thought of as the universal and the hard facts, conventions as the local and the soft facts of art.

Perhaps you recall the discussion of this subject in the *Cratylus,* Socrates refereeing at first, then refuting Hermogenes' argument that names are not attached to things by nature but are conventions of the users. I confess that as far as my art is concerned I agree with Hermogenes, even though modern philology opposes him, holding that word conventions are anything but arbitrary and that all names possess "echoic value"; and modern physics as well, if I understand anything of what Dr. Oppenheimer means by "prejudices of nature." In art, the agreements of the users, the mutual understanding of the parties to the artistic transaction, are enough, it seems to me, or at any rate they are all the artist need bother about. Profound derivations in nature are not his affair, and nature itself is only another convention to him.

QUESTION: Why does the rapidly increasing speed with which conventions are modified disturb me?

ANSWER: Because like all old men I am portentous (though prescient is the way old men prefer to think of themselves). Nevertheless, from where I stand (and my geography may be at fault), the community of criteria which has always existed somewhere in the background appears to be crumbling. Now, you may say that this does not matter, that posterity will sort the sheep from the goats, but to me such an answer is complacent. I have no confidence in the justice of posterity and have never understood the logic of the argument that though what is may be wrong, the consecration of it through time will make it right. To me all histories are deterministic. They offer not "what was" but a choice governed by the determinations, conscious and unconscious, of the choosers. I have lived long enough myself to have known a few of these histories of my own music, and to have seen the complexion put upon the very same pieces turn from Revolutionary red to Establishment gray, though, of course, the music was guilty only of reordering the conditions of its environment, of creating reaction and being reacted upon in turn according to laws of social biology that the historians did not take into account.

QUESTION: Are changes in convention brought about in a similar manner?

ANSWER: I suppose that a kind of biological process must take place, the succession of modifications at some point producing a new species, and that the metaphor might be extended to describe electronically fabricated sound as a mutation. But this is picture language, no more, and therefore a contribution to the semantic mess.

QUESTION: Where are the greater semantic obstructions, between myself and my audience, or between myself and my colleagues?

ANSWER: They are about equal, I imagine. At any rate, I seem to be about equally estranged from my youngest and oldest competitors.

QUESTION: And how do I envisage my audience today?

ANSWER: It has no visage for me, which is why I no longer have any audience in mind when I compose. Though audiences exist for my past works, they have yet to be developed for my present ones. I deplore this breach, but unlike some of my more "socially conscious" colleagues, I do not believe that it can be closed by a rapprochement in a musically backward direction. To me, any attempt to return to past safeties is as futile as the proposal a few years ago to return to "conventional" (still another meaning!) pre H- or A-bombs. We can neither put back the clock nor slow down our forward speed, and since we are already flying pilotless, on instrument controls, it is even too late to ask where we are going.

QUESTION: Finally, how do I see myself in relation to the youth of today?

ANSWER: The youngest generation is not very respectful of age, and younger composers tend to regard me with about as much interest as speeding motorists give to a discarded automobile in one of those above-ground roadside graveyards. I do not mind the relegation, though, and I have not become cynical (well, not very) observing each year's crop of these youths as they arrive and unpack their suitcases full of, or so it seems for a while, bright new ideas. We—these young people and myself—are a necessary equation, and so are the two of us, your seventeen and my eighty-three. Together we make a perfect total.

RUBE GOLDBERG

Don't Brush Off All the Old Rules

Reuben Lucius Goldberg, better known as Rube, was born on the Fourth of July eighty-three years ago in San Francisco; he began to draw at four, could hardly wait until he was grown up to turn professional cartoonist. His zany drawings made him one of our most famed funny men by the time he was in his twenties. Two years ago Rube quit cartooning to start all over again as a sculptor. Webster's Dictionary defines "Rube Goldberg" as an adjective meaning "accomplishing by extremely complex roundabout means what actually or seemingly could be done simply."

I believe the desire to be independent, to be somebody in your own right, is the bridge that carries you over from teen-age cloudiness to the clearer area of maturity. Just how can this bridge be spanned? There are many tollgates to this bridge, one of which you might enter through sheer talent and good fortune. But more often you enter the others through indecision and lack of a definite purpose. It doesn't really matter too much as long as you reach the other side with a conscious sense of the future. From the age of four I wanted to draw. I kept on drawing through my high school years. I bought all the magazines and newspapers I could lay my hands on and studied the styles of the different cartoonists and illustrators. There wasn't an artist whose name and style I did not know. I copied many of them in the hope I could find a style of my own. I loved the smell of paper and ink.

But when it came time to go to college, through deference to my father's wishes, I took a course in mining engineering. (I rebelled when he first suggested that I go to West Point.) I kept on drawing through my college years and practiced my engineering profession for about six months after graduation. I knew I had gone through the wrong tollgate and was determined to get back on the right road. So I took a job on a newspaper at eight dollars a week sweeping out the art department and drawing cartoons every day for three months only to find them in the wastebasket the next day. Finally the city editor gave me an assignment to cover a prep-school football game. I got all my pens and paper and reference pictures laid out on my desk so I would not be delayed when I came back after the game.

When I returned, all the members of the art department were out to dinner. My desk was empty and the drawer was nailed up. They had put all my drawing materials inside. I went out to the composing room, got a hammer and nails, and nailed up every desk in the room, including the boss's. Then I went home. The next day I returned expecting to be fired. Instead, I was greeted with smiles. My spunk in the midst of a crucial test had won them over. It wasn't exactly courage that caused me to fight back. I believe it was desperation born of determination to be somebody in my own right among the other artists.

Determination is an old-fashioned quality that keeps you going when disappointments and heartaches stand in your way like black ogres to block your progress.

Today the air around us is filled with new terms that are designed to brush off the stale idioms of another day. You automatically assume a posture of sophistication when you toss off gems like *corn, in, out, camp, pop, op*

and the high-sounding varieties of psychiatric nomen-
clature. If you're not *hip* to all these terms you are sitting
in a basket of stale fruit. These isms and fads are not dis-
tasteful to me. In fact, I like to use some of them myself.
But they do not supplant the old-fashioned truths or relegate them to the limbo of staleness.

A Rembrandt is not stale. Dickens is not stale. The
Grand Canyon, the Taj Mahal, the Chartres cathedral
never get stale. Monumental things like pictures or books
or the great wonders of nature or character or decency
never get stale.

A long time ago I sat at a school meeting with John D.
Rockefeller, Jr. (the father of Nelson and Winthrop and
the others). Mr. Rockefeller was asked to give his formula
for raising children. He stood up, cleared his throat and
said with a wry smile, "It is very simple. Just give them
a good mother." Then he sat down.

This, of course, was his way of saying that parental
guidance is the prime force in shaping a child's character.
But unfortunately, all parents are not equipped with the
proper tools of guidance. It seems to me somewhere along
the line there is enough love to help a normal youngster
do a little of his own guiding. Placing the complete blame
on parents when a teen-ager goes wrong is, in itself, getting a little stale. To me it should be a fifty-fifty deal.

As long as the hoary old pundit is sounding off, let me
inject another thought. Young people are carried away by
their enthusiasm for well-known personalities. They want
to be like Richard Burton, Jack Dempsey, John F. Kennedy, Paul Getty and the man who runs the candy store
on the corner. God, somehow, made only one of each
without revealing the real secret of his success. If you
emulate your hero's outward qualities without knowing
what really makes him tick, you can at best be only a
carbon copy. If you need a model to strive for, take a
composite with all the virtues that would be impossible
for one person to possess. If you can acquire ten percent
of these, you'll be doing a pretty good job.

As I suggested before, determination is the motor that keeps Sammy, Joe, Charlie and Fred running. In a recent interview a successful artist remarked facetiously, "I do it for money." Of course he did not mean this. He knew very well that a good job takes so much of yourself there is little room, while performing it, to think of the ultimate reward. Quality comes first whether you are an artist, a banker or a ditchdigger. Think of the money during the coffee break, while out on the golf course or when the finance man comes to collect on the special hi-fi you had installed in the study. But not while you are performing your job.

The rocking chair is beginning to creak. But the old pundit has one parting thought before he goes for the oil can to ease up the joints. I admire young people who are fired with unquenchable zeal to make the world a better place in which to live. They demonstrate against injustice and plead for the rights of minorities and rail against political corruption and chicanery. This takes plenty of time and energy and will eventually result in needed reforms.

But in the meantime, while waiting for the creeping utopia to arrive, you, the avid teen-ager, who are now through the tollgate and on your way to the future, should not neglect to improve *yourself*. If all else fails you will have at least contributed one good individual to a troubled world.

EILEEN FARRELL

Take Courage!

Eileen Farrell, whose dramatic soprano has thrilled audiences throughout Europe as well as the United States, completely refutes anyone's hackneyed notion of what makes an opera singer tick. Besides singing recitals and grand opera—she made her debut at the New York Metropolitan Opera House in Gluck's Alcestis *in 1960—she has guested on TV in such programs as "The Jimmy Dean Show" and sung the blues as a replacement for Louis Armstrong at the Spoleto Festival in Italy. Her recordings are available on London (her latest: "Songs America Loves"), Angel, Columbia and RCA Victor. She is the proud mother of two teen-agers, a girl of thirteen and a boy of nineteen.*

Dear Teen-age Audience:

Even though I address you collectively, I don't believe in your collective existence. As I go around the country for opera and concert engagements (and here at home in New York too), I hear all kinds of loose talk about teen-agers, about "your" problems, "your" attitudes and various choruses of lamentation or rejoicing about "your" faults or virtues. As if you were just a great, shapeless mass.

207   Talk like that strikes me as the kind of nonsense not

likely to result in anything constructive. I don't see you as one single group. I don't think you've cornered the problem market. And I'm quite sure there's as much variation in attitudes among you as among any other age group. How else could we read about some of you demonstrating against the war in Vietnam, and others demonstrating against the demonstrators? About the only thing you all have in common is the fact that you're between thirteen and nineteen—and that's my only excuse for starting this letter "Dear Teen-age Audience."

The worst thing about thinking of you collectively is not that it won't work—and it won't—but the effect it could have on *you*. In-depth techniques of advertising, publicity and propaganda have developed in us generally a tendency to accept the reiterated word without too much resistance. And the constantly repeated references to teen-agers today as a group, of whom what is true of one is true of all, may succeed in convincing you, yourselves, that you really are more members of a group than individuals within it. This could be a tragedy, not only for you, but for the world, for the important contributions to mankind have always been made by individuals.

Certainly you have problems—more profound ones than how to be popular or get into college or find a job with a future. And the solution, as I see it, might be summed up in one word—courage! Somehow you must cultivate the courage to try, the courage to look failure in the face and not be bowled over by it, and to explore the world and people outside the boundaries you now live within. How do I dare offer you such a sweeping generalization in the face of having just said you are individuals and not a group? Because I believe that courage is the basic requisite for solving any problem, for any age. I remember reading somewhere an article which likened life to a vast, circular room filled with a constantly renewed multitude of people. Leading from this room were countless archways, through which could be seen paths that led away in different directions. Some people left the room through one archway, some through another. Some, finding the path they'd chosen to their liking, continued on it. Others, not happy at what they found, but ashamed to return to the room and admit they'd made a poor choice, stuck with it, despite joy-killing doubts and reservations. Still others returned to the room to try another archway, and if necessary another, until they found one leading to a path that seemed to promise what they were seeking. But some people, the writer went on, stayed in that room all of their lives and never found the courage to leave it. They lived safely enough until they died, but who's to say if they had a Life?

When I came across this little parable, it seemed to have a special significance for me. Because before I studied singing, I studied art. My brother was an artist and I thought it must be wonderful to be able to create something visible to others that communicated to them one's inner thoughts and feelings. Music had always been part of our home. My parents were both professional singers and my mother, who was then a voice teacher, was also teaching me how to sing. But, possibly just because I'd always been familiar with it, music didn't capture my imagination as a way of life at that point, as art, the unfamiliar, did. So I studied art, only to discover I had no creativeness to bring to it. I could copy well, and I could do the mechanical tasks of adapting the designs of others to sketches necessary to translate them into fabric or wallpaper designs. But I could see that my attempts to create designs of my own were echoes of the ideas of others.

After I graduated from high school, my mother took me to New York to sing for a friend of hers who had been a concert and opera singer, and who was now teaching voice. The teacher agreed with my mother that I should stay in New York and study singing with her, and I thought, "Well, I will give this singing idea a whirl, since as an artist, I'm never going to be more than a good draughtsman." To my joy, I discovered in the interpretive art of singing an outlet for the expression of my feelings and a way of communication that had eluded me in the creative medium of painting and drawing. And that is how I embarked on my vocal studies. How much I would have lost if I'd been afraid to change or had felt that doing so indicated some lack of character!

All right. So I had found a way of communicating. But could a make a career as a singer? Facing myself honestly, I knew I lacked the kind of physical glamor generally associated with a performing career. But I told myself that needn't matter. If I had the talent, and would work to develop it, I could make it on that. I worked hard, and the voice did develop, and suddenly I found myself with the beginnings of a career. After several auditions for radio I became a featured soloist on a coast-to-coast program, and eventually I had my own program. That made me known to such a wide audience that I began to be sought for concerts, and a whole new area began to open up to me.

If I had let myself be limited by the lack of a stream-lined figure or the sultry looks of a movie siren, I might never have ventured into opera, but instead would have stayed invisibly in radio or confined myself to the concert stage, where I could appear as "Eileen Farrell, soprano," in my own personality without having to persuade audiences that I was also Tosca, Santuzza, Leonora or Medea, as the case might be. But by this time I'd discovered I had a flair for the theatrical, and I told myself again that talent could carry me through.

Now I don't tell you all this as a success story. Success. It's one of those big words. It means so many things to so many people that in the abstract it means nothing. As a concept, it varies with those who woo it, and if at this point in your lives you think of it most simply as "getting somewhere," I must take issue with you. In my book, you're putting the cart before the horse. For I believe that only those who are on the road to being a success as human beings can hope to "get" anywhere.

What do I mean by a successful human being? I mean someone who's in touch with as much of life as possible, and who isn't the victim of timid aspirations. The world is full of reporters, for instance, who never got the job—because they were so sure they wouldn't, they never even applied for it. Why? What's so bad about being turned down? It leaves you free to try somewhere else. And besides, you might be accepted.

I view you all with great affection, sympathy and interest. But I worry about you too, because you seem to me to limit yourselves. Many of you reject things out of hand because they are "square"—or you go along with other things uncritically because they're "in." You have discovered the joys of belonging—to your own particular, congenial group, but you have little contact with teens outside it. It seems to me you lose a lot this way—and so do those from whom you shut yourself off. You may love folk songs but shudder at the idea of going to a concert, or vice versa. Why? It's all music. Or you may be against others of you whose political attitudes are different from yours, without even knowing why they hold them.

Whenever it manifests itself, this kind of exclusivity seems regrettable to me. The successful human being, as I see him, is willing, even eager, to expose himself to new experiences and ideas. He welcomes contact not only with those who agree with him, but with those who don't —not necessarily to persuade them to his way of thinking (though that's always a possibility) but to learn something about theirs. That's the only way to replace prejudices that create fear—with the knowledge born of conviction that gives courage. And with courage, everything is possible!